EDWARD'S
MENAGERIE
——— BIRDS ———

#edsanimals

EDWARD'S
MENAGERIE
— BIRDS —

Kerry Lord

DAVID & CHARLES

www.davidandcharles.com

CONTENTS

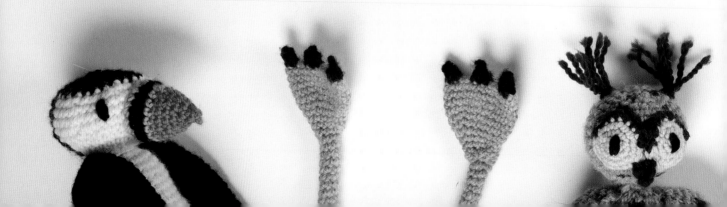

INTRODUCTION

Edward's Menagerie: Birds is a continuation of an on-going project of a self-taught newbie crocheter, as hooked as the rest of you and with an imagination ignited by a toddler. It turns out that crochet, and crocheting *Edward's Menagerie* creatures in particular, is strangely addictive. Don't say I didn't warn you!

Since I first conceived of Bridget the Elephant, and worked through the other forty *Edward's Menagerie* mammals I have had a flock of birds flapping around at the back of my mind. It would seem that the more animals you crochet, the more frequent your trips to the zoo become, and ultimately you start simplifying and admiring every knobbly knee you see.

Birds by their very appearance were always going to be a bit more fiddly than the *Edward's Menagerie* mammals. That gawky yet elegant avian character lends itself to small rounds and detailed shaping. I knew it would be more of a challenge – new shapes, big features and bright colours – but what I didn't know was that it could take TOFT off in a whole new colourful direction.

Sophia the Flamingo was the first bird off my hook, and her floppy neck and oversized crooked beak gave her a big personality that instantly proved a hit with Edward. If you are a complete beginner to crochet and *Edward's Menagerie*, then start with the level one birds; a shape like Ernest the Canary is a perfect initiation project. In *Edward's Menagerie: Birds* the projects are arranged by difficulty, not only into levels, but also within that level, so you can progress through the pages on to those that require a bit more concentration, like Anik the Snowy Owl. From Vince the kooky Booby to Elizabeth the indulgent Dodo (I couldn't resist) this book should have something for everyone to cuddle and have a giggle with.

The patterns in this book are designed for you and your friends and family to enjoy and are for private use only. I can't wait to see photos of your menagerie birds; make sure you share them using the hashtag **#edsanimals**, so that I can enjoy looking at them, and you can see everyone else's, too.

Turning my studio into a crocheted aviary has been a pleasure and I know you'll find making these birds just as much fun and as addictive as Edward's other menagerie animals. So, now that there's another animal class in the bag, it only leaves the question: where next? Answers strapped to Dora's leg please.

Enjoy,

[signature]

HOW TO USE THIS BOOK

Please don't feel that you have to practise, learn or master the *Technicals* section of this book before you dive head-first into a project. Flick to the back as you go along to acquire, double check or refresh your skills as you work through your first bird.

Edward's Menagerie: Birds has been divided into three levels to indicate how many techniques are used in the making of that bird. I have added an 'optional' fourth digit onto some of the Level 1 birds. Adding this 'toe' requires that you use a slip stitch technique onto the surface of your already crocheted fabric to create a root from which to build rounds (see *Technicals*). Although simple once you get the hang of it, complete beginners might find it a bit awkward, and so it can simply be left off (remember that you can always revisit your early projects and add the toes at a later date once you are feeling more confident!).

Although the Level 3 birds still use very simple stitch techniques, many of them require demanding colour changing patterns, which those new to crochet might find difficult to keep track of when counting increasing and decreasing patterns at the same time. Try your hook out with a Level 1 bird first and then you'll quickly progress onto the penguins!

LEVEL 1

Birds using only chain, slip stitch, double crochet, and with basic colour changes moving cleanly from colour one to colour two. Instructions for this can be found in the Technicals section.

LEVEL 2

Birds for which you will need to learn the loop/fur stitch (see Working the Stitches in the Technicals section).

LEVEL 3

Birds that require complex colour changing and splitting techniques. You will need all of the techniques in the Technicals section, including slip stitch traverse for building a root and crochet into both sides of a chain.

The birds in this book are of a feather and share common body shapes. You will need to refer to the *Standard Forms* pages when making any of them. You will notice that these pages have a black tab to help you find them quickly when you are working through a pattern. After you have made one bird, you will pick up the pattern quickly (and become very familiar with your six times table!).

To keep each pattern simple and concise, I have omitted the stuffing and the sewing-up instructions, as these are common to all. Please refer to the *Sewing and Stuffing* pages in the *Technicals* section before you start, so that you are aware of the correct order and the place in the pattern to do this.

The patterns all use British crochet terminology and common crochet abbreviations. US conversions and full explanations can be found in the *Technicals* section.

YARNS & OTHER MATERIALS

MY YARN STORY

I have had the privilege of growing up on a British alpaca farm in a picturesque area of rural Warwickshire, England, named Toft. Toft is a place where my son Edward – for whom this menagerie is named – will be able to make weekly visits, and where he can enjoy taking part in the daily rituals of farming these beautiful camelids.

I commissioned the first batch of TOFT alpaca yarn back in 2006, and at the time I had never knitted or crocheted a stitch. I rapidly started to enjoy knitting and found particular pleasure in designing and wearing clothing from this beautiful yarn. Then, in 2012, when I was pregnant for the first time, I picked up a hook and a few months later *Edward's Menagerie* was born.

TOFT has grown to become a renowned luxury yarn brand committed to British manufacture and superior quality alpaca and wool yarns, and these are now stocked in local yarn shops across the world.

MY YARN CHOICE

Edward's Menagerie: Birds has been crocheted entirely in TOFT yarn, and in doing so I have stretched and reinvented TOFT's all-natural palette reputation. For this collection of bird patterns I have created my own pure wool yarns dyed in the UK to very specific shades. These are colours that although dyed are still (albeit sometimes surprisingly) true to nature's colours. Although many of the birds use the pops of bright colour, the collection is rooted in the rich natural tones that characterize the TOFT brand. The creation of *Edward's Menagerie: Birds* has pushed the TOFT brand in a new direction to ensure that the quality of the yarn remains integral to the appeal and finish of the animal or bird. *Edward's Menagerie* animals in TOFT yarn are supple, soft and above all they wear in, getting better and better with every cuddle.

Naturally, I recommend using TOFT yarn to guarantee that your birds look and feel just like mine, but the patterns will work in any other non-fancy spun yarn. The resulting birds will vary drastically should you choose to work up a bleached white acrylic dove or an owl in bright pink cotton, but the patterns will work if you match your hook size to your yarn and check that your tension makes a dense, crisp fabric.

I hope these patterns inspire you to experience the pleasure of indulging in a luxury yarn. They are small projects to ignite, amuse and inspire, whether you are bringing one of these patterns to life for yourself, a friend or family member.

YARN COLOURS

When I began crocheting *Edward's Menagerie: Birds* I was lucky enough to fall upon the most perfect flamingo pink. I happily crocheted away taking for granted that when I needed to source a 'beak' yellow and 'foot' orange I'd find what I was looking for. I was wrong. There began another long search and journey to find the perfect shade of yellow, and then orange, and green...

Even the most humble birds are more colourful than you think! The common mallard sports a total of seven colours and the often-overlooked turkey tops the charts weighing in at no less than eight colours to complete him. The birds in this book use far more colours than anything else I have ever made or designed, and in making them I have discovered the pleasure in highlighting the neutrals I know so well with bright flashes. The only drawback to this is you need a couple of balls of yarn in different colours to get started, but then I'm sure they will all come in handy as I dare you to try and make only one...

YOU WILL NEED

TO MAKE JUST ONE, OR INDEED ALL, OF THE ANIMALS IN THIS BOOK, THE REQUIREMENTS LIST IS THE SAME:

Yarn in appropriate colours and quantities (see *Sizing*)

Black contrast yarn for eyes

One hook in an appropriate size to the yarn being used (see *Sizing*)

Stuffing material (not a lot!)

Sewing needle

Scissors

NATURALS

1 CREAM: a rich natural white from unbleached fleeces

2 OATMEAL: a peachy soft and light fawn

3 STONE: a gorgeous warm blush grey from natural mixed fleeces of white, black and fawn

4 CAMEL: a warm, tempting cookie-dough fawn

5 FUDGE: a rich ginger fawn

6 CHESTNUT: a stunning polished red-brown

7 MUSHROOM: an intriguing natural shade of cool-brown

8 SILVER: a soft and sophisticated light grey from mixed fleeces of black and white

9 STEEL: a bold, defined mid grey with almost blue undertones

10 CHARCOAL: a deep grey softer alternative to true black

COLOURS

11 BLACK: an over-dyed true black with a real depth and lustre that is perfect for eyes

12 YELLOW: the perfect strength of warm mustard

13 ORANGE: a rich surprisingly bright colour to see in nature

14 GREEN: an almost iridescent deep forest green

15 LIME: a soft but sour light green

16 PINK: a perfect self-consciously blushing pink

17 BLUE: an electrifying shade of bright blue

MATERIALS FOR STUFFING

I have chosen to stuff these birds with a synthetic high-loft polyester toy filling, despite their 100 per cent natural yarn outer. Rather than this being a contradiction, experience has taught me that natural wool stuffing tends to compact over time and leads to lumpy and saggy animals. The synthetic stuffing also ensures that the birds are fully hand-washable, and come out looking quite revitalized after a cool cycle in your washing machine.

MATERIALS FOR FACES

I have used black yarn to sew on all the bird's eyes. As a result of the success of the *Edward's Menagerie* collection, TOFT has now developed a lustrous over-dyed black, perfect for adding a subtle glint to the eyes. On the birds with black heads I have used charcoal yarn to add the eyes. This is something I have debated over long and hard, and one penguin in particular must have suffered at least twenty ocular transplants before settling on his dark grey eyes.

SIZING

The standard *Edward's Menagerie* bird is worked in Double Knitting (DK) weight yarn on a 3mm crochet hook (for US crocheters: light worsted/8ply yarn on a C2 or D3 hook). The beauty of the pattern is that you never need to change the hook size and you only need one tool to make all forty animals featured in this book!

All the figures given in the tables are approximate and based on my experience working with TOFT yarns. You could make any one of these animals in any thickness of yarn, but with the Level 2 and 3 animals you might find some parts become quite demanding when worked in very fine yarns. Thicker yarns and bigger hooks may suit beginners best, as it is easier to see (and count) the stitches.

These quantities are based on using TOFT yarns. If you use another brand, the quantities required may vary significantly, depending on the fibre composition and spinning specifications of the yarn. Birds that use the loop/fur stitch or chain loops to add detailed plumage will take considerably more yarn than others.

Your hook size needs to be selected based on yarn thickness but also considering your own personal tension. Adjust your hook size to accommodate your tension and thickness of yarn ensuring that your fabric is dense: if it is too loose your stuffing will show through; if it is too tight your animals will be stiff and hard to crochet. The tension measurements given here are approximate and measured over standard double crochet stitches worked in a spiral.

The sizes given in the boxes are for Barney the Owl, measured from top to toes. The length of the birds varies subject to neck, leg and crest additions.

INTERNATIONAL TERMS

I have used British English crochet terms throughout. 'Double crochet' (dc) is the same as the American English 'Single crochet' (sc). For clarification on which stitch this refers to, see the instructions for double crochet in the *Technicals* section. All other abbreviations are the same in both British and American terms.

SMALL		
YARN WEIGHT	UK	FINE
	US/AU	SPORT/4PLY
QUANTITY	G	30–50
	OZ	1–1¾
HOOK SIZE	MM	1.75
	US/AU	n/a
FINISHED SIZE	CM	18
	IN	7
TENSION	CM	2 x 2cm = 6 sts x 7 rows
	IN	¾ x ¾in = 6 sts x 7 rows

STANDARD		
YARN WEIGHT	UK	DK
	US/AU	LIGHT WORSTED/8PLY
QUANTITY	G	60–100
	OZ	2–3½
HOOK SIZE	MM	3
	US/AU	C2/D3
FINISHED SIZE	CM	28
	IN	11
TENSION	CM	3 x 3cm = 6 sts x 7 rows
	IN	1¼ x 1¼in = 6 sts x 7 rows

LARGE		
YARN WEIGHT	UK	ARAN
	US/AU	WORSTED/10PLY
QUANTITY	G	300–400
	OZ	10–14
HOOK SIZE	MM	5
	US/AU	H8
FINISHED SIZE	CM	40
	IN	15¾
TENSION	CM	5 x 5cm = 6 sts x 7 rows
	IN	2 x 2in = 6 sts x 7 rows

GIANT		
YARN WEIGHT	UK	CHUNKY
	US/AU	BULKY/12PLY
QUANTITY	G	600–1000
	OZ	20–35
HOOK SIZE	MM	8
	US/AU	L11
FINISHED SIZE	CM	60
	IN	23½
TENSION	CM	7 x 7cm = 6 sts x 7 rows
	IN	2¾ x 2¾in = 6 sts x 7 rows

STANDARD FORMS

For this collection of bird patterns I have developed standard forms to cover certain shapes which are repeated within the patterns. I have labelled the parts as some patterns will require that you extend or reduce a section and this should make it really easy to visualize the subtle change to the standard form.

When you have completed a part, unless it is otherwise stated, thread the yarn through the remaining stitches, pull tight and secure by sewing through the part and around a stitch a couple of times. When making each part, ensure that when you start or finish you leave yourself a length of yarn to sew that part onto the others as this will make your life easier when sewing up the bird.

BODY/NECK/HEAD

In the patterns I have not stated when you should stuff parts. My advice is that anything that involves a colour change or an extended neck should be stuffed before you reduce to the neck as it is a very hard job pushing that stuffing through once you have completed the whole body/neck/head standard form.

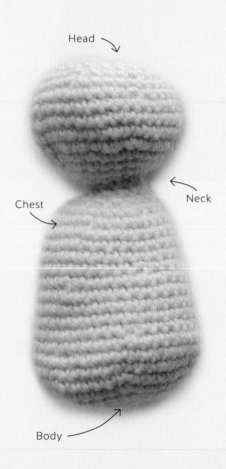

Head

Neck

Chest

Body

Begin by dc6 into foundation ring (see *Technicals*)

Rnd 1 (dc2 into next st) 6 times (12)

Rnd 2 (dc1, dc2 into next st) 6 times (18)

Rnd 3 (dc2, dc2 into next st) 6 times (24)

Rnd 4 (dc3, dc2 into next st) 6 times (30)

Rnd 5 (dc4, dc2 into next st) 6 times (36)

Rnd 6 (dc5, dc2 into next st) 6 times (42)

Rnds 7–9 dc (3 rnds)

Rnd 10 (dc5, dc2tog) 6 times (36)

Rnds 11–14 dc (4 rnds)

Rnd 15 (dc4, dc2tog) 6 times (30)

Rnds 16–19 dc (4 rnds)

Rnd 20 (dc3, dc2tog) 6 times (24)

Rnd 21 dc

Rnd 22 (dc2tog) 9 times, dc 6 (15)

Rnd 23 (dc2tog) 5 times, dc 5 (10)

NECK

Rnd 24 dc

HEAD

Rnd 25 (dc2 into next st) 10 times (20)

Rnd 26 (dc3, dc2 into next st) 5 times (25)

Rnd 27 (dc4, dc2 into next st) 5 times (30)

Rnd 28 (dc2, dc2 into next st) 10 times (40)

Rnds 29–31 dc (3 rnds)

Rnd 32 (dc8, dc2tog) 4 times (36)

Rnd 33 dc

Rnd 34 (dc4, dc2tog) 6 times (30)

Rnd 35 (dc3, dc2tog) 6 times (24)

Rnd 36 (dc2, dc2tog) 6 times (18)

Rnd 37 dc

Rnd 38 (dc2tog) 9 times (9)

Rnd 39 (dc1, dc2tog) 3 times (6)

LEGS

Most birds' legs are skinny, long and a little bit bony. Although you may find the small rounds a bit fiddly to begin with, it will get easier, but please ensure that you are working right-side out (RS vs. WS see *Technicals* for details). You will find it almost impossible to work a six stitch round inside out and you won't be able to flip it to the right side at the end as you can with larger parts.

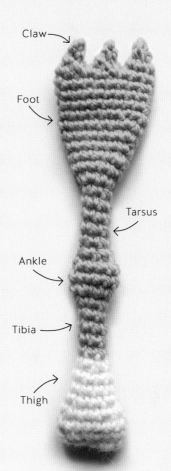

PADDLING LEG

THIGH
Ch15 and sl st to join into a circle

Rnds 1-2 dc (2 rnds)

Rnd 3 (dc3, dc2tog) 3 times (12)

Rnd 4 (dc2, dc2tog) 3 times (9)

Rnds 5-6 dc (2 rnds)

Rnd 7 (dc1, dc2tog) 3 times (6)

TIBIA
Rnds 8-12 dc (5 rnds)

ANKLE
Rnd 13 (dc2 into next st) 6 times (12)

Rnds 14-15 dc (2 rnds)

Rnd 16 (dc2tog) 6 times (6)

TARSUS
Rnds 17-22 dc (6 rnds)

FOOT
Rnd 23 (dc2 into next st) 6 times (12)

Rnd 24 dc

Rnd 25 (dc5, dc2 into next st) twice (14)

Rnd 26 (dc6, dc2 into next st) twice (16)

Rnd 27 (dc7, dc2 into next st) twice (18)

Rnds 28-32 dc (5 rnds)

CLAWS
Split into three 6 st rnds and work each as follows:

Rnd 1 dc

Rnd 2 (dc2tog) 3 times (3)

Fold the top flat and dc across the top, first stuffing the thigh if required.

SWIMMING LEG

THIGH
Ch16 and sl st to join into a circle

Rnds 1-5 dc (5 rnds)

Rnd 6 (dc2, dc2tog) 4 times (12)

Rnd 7 (dc1, dc2tog) 4 times (8)

TIBIA
Rnds 8-9 dc (2 rnds)

ANKLE
Rnd 10 (dc1, dc2 into next st) 4 times (12)

Rnds 11-12 dc (2 rnds)

Rnd 13 (dc1, dc2tog) 4 times (8)

TARSUS
Rnds 14-20 dc (7 rnds)

FOOT
Rnd 21 (dc2 into next st) 8 times (16)

Rnd 22 dc

Rnd 23 (dc7, dc2 into next st) twice (18)

Rnd 24 (dc8, dc2 into next st) twice (20)

Rnd 25 dc

Rnd 26 (dc9, dc2 into next st) twice (22)

Rnd 27 dc

Rnd 28 (dc10, dc2 into next st) twice (24)

Rnds 29-31 dc (3 rnds)

CLAWS
Split into three 8st branches and work each as follows:

Rnd 1 dc

Rnd 2 (dc2tog) 4 times (4)

Rnd 3 (dc2tog) twice (2)

Fold the top flat and dc across the top, first stuffing the thigh if required.

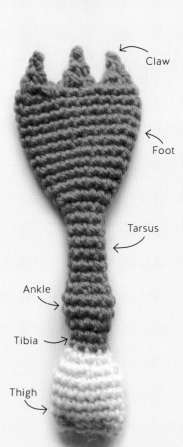

Digit

Foot

Thigh

CLIMBING LEG

Ch12 and sl st to join into a circle

Rnds 1–8 dc (8 rnds)

Rnd 9 (dc2tog) 6 times (6)

Rnds 10–18 dc (9 rnds)

FOOT

See *Working the Stitches, Chain Split* in the *Technicals* section

Next, ch6 and sl st across the other side of the rnd. This 6 st ch forms a foundation chain which you will work both sides of to create rnds that split off in both directions at 90 degree angles from the leg.

Rnd 1 dc8 (6 into chain and 2 into the bottom rnd of leg)

Rnd 2 (dc1, dc2 into next st) 4 times (12)

Split into two rnds of 6 sts and work each as follows:

DIGITS

Rnds 1– 4 dc (4 rnds)

Rnd 5 (dc2, dc2 into next st) twice (8)

Rnds 6–7 dc (2 rnds)

Rnd 8 (dc2, dc2tog) twice (6)

Rnd 9 (dc1, dc2tog) twice (4)

Rnd 10 (dc2tog) twice (2)

Next, rejoin yarn on other side of the foundation chain and repeat as above

Fold the top flat and dc across the top, first stuffing the thigh if required.

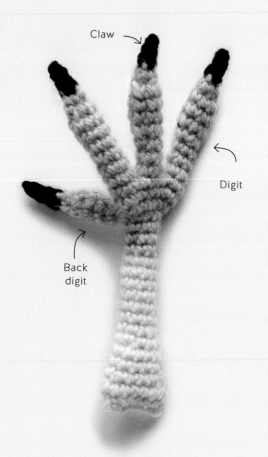

Claw

Digit

Back digit

GRASPING LEG

Ch15 and sl st to join into a circle

Rnds 1–2 dc (2 rnds)

Rnd 3 (dc3, dc2tog) 3 times (12)

Rnds 4–5 dc (2 rnds)

Rnd 6 (dc2, dc2tog) 3 times (9)

Rnds 7–12 dc (6 rnds)

Rnd 13 dc7, dc2tog (8)

Rnds 14–17 dc (4 rnds)

Rnd 18 (dc2 into next st) 8 times (16)

Rnd 19 (dc 7, dc2 into next st) twice (18)

Split into three 6 st rnds and work each as follows:

DIGITS

Rnds 1–4 dc (4 rnds)

Rnd 5 dc5, dc2 into next st (7)

Rnd 6 dc

Rnd 7 dc6, dc2 into next (8)

Rnd 8 dc

Rnd 9 (dc2tog) 4 times (4)

Change to contrast colour if desired to work

CLAWS

Rnd 10 dc

Rnd 11 (dc2tog) twice (2)

BACK (OPTIONAL) DIGIT

Sl st traverse a 6 st root on the back of the foot (see *Adding Details* in *Technicals*) and work as follows:

Rnds 1–3 dc (3 rnds)

Rnd 4 (dc1, dc2tog) twice (4)

Change to contrast colour if desired to work

CLAW

Rnd 5 dc

Rnd 6 (dc2tog) twice (2)

Fold the top flat and dc across the top, first stuffing the thigh if required.

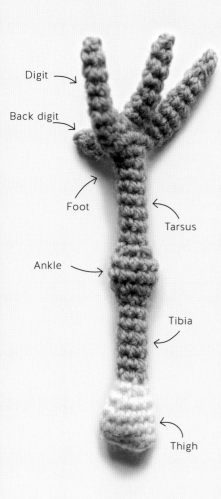

Digit

Back digit

Foot

Tarsus

Ankle

Tibia

Thigh

PERCHING LEG

Refer to the diagram in the *Technicals* section

THIGH

Ch12 and sl st to join into a circle

Rnds 1–3 dc (3 rnds)

Rnd 4 (dc2, dc2tog) 3 times (9)

Rnd 5 (dc1, dc2tog) 3 times (6)

TIBIA

Rnds 6–12 dc (7 rnds)

ANKLE

Rnd 13 (dc2 into next st) 6 times (12)

Rnds 14–15 dc (2 rnds)

Rnd 16 (dc2tog) 6 times (6)

TARSUS

Rnds 17–24 dc (8 rnds)

FOOT

Rnd 25 (dc2 into next st) 6 times (12)

Rnd 26 (dc1, dc2 into next st) 6 times (18)

Split into three 6st branches and rejoin and work each as follows:

DIGITS

Rnds 1–3 dc

Rnd 4 dc2tog, dc4 (5)

Rnds 5–6 dc

Rnd 7 dc2tog, dc3 (4)

BACK (OPTIONAL) DIGIT

See *Adding Details* in *Technicals*

Slip stitch traverse a 6 st root on the back of the foot (see *Adding Details* in *Technicals*) and work as follows:

Rnd 1 dc

Rnd 2 dc2tog, dc4 (5)

Rnds 3–4 dc

Rnd 5 dc2tog, dc3 (4)

Fold the top flat and dc across the top, first stuffing the thigh if required.

WADDLING LEG

THIGH

Ch30 and sl st to join into a circle

Rnds 1–4 dc (4 rnds)

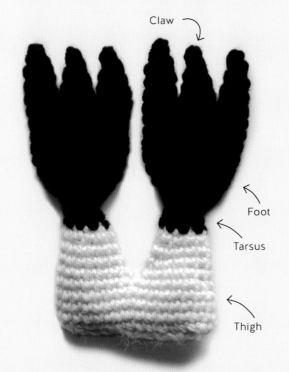

Claw

Foot

Tarsus

Thigh

Split into two 15 st rnds and work each as follows:

Rnd 1 dc (15)

Rnd 2 dc13, dc2tog (14)

Rnd 3 dc12, dc2tog (13)

Rnd 4 dc11, dc2tog (12)

Rnd 5 (dc4, dc2tog) twice (10)

TARSUS

Rnd 6 (dc3, dc2tog) twice (8)

Rnd 7 dc

Rnd 8 (dc2, dc2tog) twice (6)

FOOT

Rnd 9 (dc2 into next st) 6 times (12)

Rnd 10 (dc1, dc2 into next st) 6 times (18)

Rnds 11–16 dc (6 rnds)

Split into three 6 st rnds and work each as follows:

Rnds 1–2 dc (2 rnds)

CLAWS

Change to black

Rnd 3 dc

Rnd 4 (dc2tog) 3 times (3)

WINGS

Please don't wade too deep into the categorizing of these wings. I am not an ornithologist and some of these flapping birds can fly and some of the soaring birds merely hover. Enjoy the fact that you can multi task while whipping up these standard forms (especially once you get onto your fifth or sixth pair).

FLYING WING

Begin by dc6 into foundation ring (see *Technicals*)

Rnd 1 (dc1, dc2 into next st) 3 times (9)

Rnd 2 dc8, dc2 into last st (10)

Rnd 3 dc

Rnd 4 dc9, dc2 into last st (11)

Rnd 5 dc

Rnd 6 dc10, dc2 into last st (12)

Rnd 7 dc

Rnd 8 dc11, dc2 into last St (13)

Rnd 9 dc

Rnd 10 dc12, dc2 into last st (14)

Rnd 11 dc

Rnd 12 (dc6, dc2 into next st) twice (16)

Rnd 13 dc2 into first st, dc14, dc2 into last st (18)

Rnd 14 dc2 into first st, dc16, dc2 into last st (20)

Rnd 15 dc2 into first st, dc18, dc2 into last st (22)

Rnd 16 dc2 into first st, dc20, dc2 into last st (24)

Rnd 17 dc2 into first st, dc22, dc2 into last st (26)

Rnds 18–21 dc (4 rnds)

Rnd 22 (dc11, dc2tog) twice (24)

Rnd 23 (dc2, dc2tog) 6 times (18)

Rnd 24 dc

Rnd 25 (dc1, dc2tog) 6 times (12)

Rnd 26 (dc2tog) 6 times (6)

SOARING WING

Begin by dc6 into foundation ring (see *Technicals*)

Rnd 1 (dc1, dc2 into next st) 3 times (9)

Rnd 2 dc8, dc2 into last st (10)

Rnd 3 dc9, dc2 into last st (11)

Rnd 4 dc10, dc2 into last st (12)

Rnd 5 dc11, dc2 into last st (13)

Rnd 6 dc12, dc2 into last st (14)

Rnd 7 dc13, dc2 into last st (15)

Rnd 8 dc14, dc2 into last st (16)

Rnd 9 dc15, dc2 into last st (17)

Rnd 10 dc16, dc2 into last st (18)

Rnd 11 dc17, dc2 into last st (19)

Rnd 12 dc18, dc2 into last st (20)

Rnd 13 dc19, dc2 into last st (21)

Rnd 14 dc20, dc2 into last st (22)

Rnd 15 dc21, dc2 into last st (23)

Rnd 16 dc22, dc2 into last st (24)

Rnd 17 dc2 into first st, dc22, dc2 into last st (26)

Rnd 18 dc2 into first st, dc24, dc2 into last st (28)

Rnd 19 dc27, dc2 into last st (29)

Rnd 20 dc28, dc2 into last st (30)

Rnd 21 (dc3, dc2tog) 6 times (24)

Rnd 22 (dc2tog) 12 times (12)

Rnd 23 (dc2tog) 6 times (6)

FLAPPING WING

Begin by dc6 into foundation ring (see *Technicals*)

Rnd 1 (dc2 into next st) 6 times (12)

Rnd 2 (dc1, dc2 into next st) 6 times (18)

Rnd 3 (dc2, dc2 into next st) 6 times (24)

Rnds 4–5 dc (2 rnds)

Rnd 6 (dc2, dc2tog) 6 times (18)

Rnds 7–8 dc (2 rnds)

Rnd 9 (dc4, dc2tog) 3 times (15)

Rnd 10 dc

Rnd 11 (dc1, dc2tog) 5 times (10)

Rnds 12–13 dc (2 rnds)

Rnd 14 (dc2tog) 5 times (5)

ORNAMENTAL WING

Begin by dc5 into foundation ring (see *Technicals*)

Rnd 1 (dc2 into next st) 5 times (10)

Rnd 2 (dc1, dc2 into next st) 5 times (15)

Rnd 3 dc

Rnd 4 (dc3, dc2tog) 3 times (12)

Rnd 5 dc

Rnd 6 (dc2, dc2tog) 3 times (9)

Rnd 7 (dc1, dc2tog) 3 times (6)

Rnd 8 (dc2tog) 3 times (3)

SWIMMING WING

LEFT WING

Working in black

Begin by dc6 into foundation ring (see *Technicals*)

Rnd 1 dc2, dc2 into next st black, dc2 into next st cream, dc2 black (8)

Rnd 2 dc3, dc2 into next st black, dc2 into next st, dc1 cream, dc2 black (10)

Rnd 3 dc4, dc2 into next st black, dc2 into next st, dc2 cream, dc2 black (12)

Rnd 4 dc5, dc2 into next st black, dc2 into next st, dc3 cream, dc2 black (14)

Rnd 5 dc6, dc2 into next st black, dc2 into next st, dc4 cream, dc2 black (16)

Rnd 6 dc7, dc2 into next st black, dc2 into next st, dc5 cream, dc2 black (18)

Rnd 7 dc8, dc2 into next st black, dc2 into next st, dc6 cream, dc2 black (20)

Rnds 8–12 dc10 black, dc8 cream, dc2 black (5 rnds)

Rnds 13–17 dc11 black, dc7 cream, dc2 black (5 rnds)

Rnd 18 dc1, (dc2tog) twice, dc6 black, dc4, (dc2tog) twice cream, dc1 black (16)

Rnd 19 dc1, (dc2tog) twice, dc4 black, dc2, (dc2tog) twice cream, dc1 black (12)

Rnd 20 dc black

Fold in half and dc across top to close.

RIGHT WING

Working in black

Begin by dc6 into foundation ring (see *Technicals*)

Rnd 1 dc1 cream, dc1, (dc2 into next st) twice, dc2 black (8)

Rnd 2 dc2 cream, dc1, (dc2 into next st) twice, dc3 black (10)

Rnd 3 dc3 cream, dc1, (dc2 into next st) twice, dc4 black (12)

Rnd 4 dc4 cream, dc1, (dc2 into next st) twice, dc5 black (14)

Rnd 5 dc5 cream, dc1, (dc2 into next st) twice, dc6 black (16)

Rnd 6 dc6 cream, dc1, (dc2 into next st) twice, dc7 black (18)

Rnd 7 dc7 cream, dc1, (dc2 into next st) twice, dc8 black (20)

Rnd 8 dc8 cream, dc12 black

Rnds 9–12 dc9 cream, dc11 black (4 rnds)

Rnds 13–17 dc1 black, dc8 cream, dc11 black (5 rnds)

Rnd 18 dc1 black, (dc2tog) twice, dc 4 cream, dc6 (dc2tog) twice, dc1 black (16)

Rnd 19 dc1, black (dc2tog) twice, dc2 cream, dc4, (dc2tog) twice, dc1 black (12)

Rnd 20 dc black

Fold in half and dc across top to close.

LEFT WING

RIGHT WING

LEVEL 1

The birds in Level 1 require knowledge of only the basics of crochet, including very simple colour changing. Cut your yarn after the change. You don't need to worry about sewing in the ends; just leave them inside the part. These birds are suitable for beginners who have read the *Technicals* section.

A few of the birds in this section will have an 'optional' fourth claw. Not taking this option is a perfect solution for a beginner to be able to successfully complete their first project using one of these patterns. For the twitchers and perfectionists amongst you, tackle the slip stitch traverse technique. It sounds much more intimidating than it is and gives a perfect finish to the foot.

CELINE
the Dove

Celine is an artist who lives in her own perfectly balanced regime; it takes a severe dose of order and discipline to balance her explosive expressions of colour. If you ever have the pleasure of meeting her you'll be soothed and calmed by her immaculate and tranquil demeanor, but once she's cooped up in her studio she creates chaos, disorder and discordant mess on her canvases. When she's not to be found channelling peace, conciliation and tranquillity (or splashing and mixing paint) she'll be knee-deep in peroxide reinstating her perfection; it's a tough job maintaining the purest shade of white.

YOU WILL NEED

Main colour: Cream

Colour two: Oatmeal

See also *You will need* list in *Yarn and Other Materials* section, and *Abbreviations*.

BODY/NECK/HEAD

Work as *standard* in cream.

LEGS

Work as *standard PERCHING* but with 6 rnds *TIBIA* and 7 rnds *TARSUS* starting in cream, colour changing to oatmeal after thigh.

WINGS

Work *standard FLYING* in cream.

BEAK

Working in cream

Ch8 and sl st to join into a circle

Rnds 1–2 dc (2 rnds)

Rnd 3 (dc2, dc2tog) twice (6)

Rnds 4–5 dc (2 rnds)

Rnd 6 (dc2tog) 3 times (3)

TAIL (made in two parts)

PART ONE:

Working in cream
Ch18 and sl st to join into a circle

Rnd 1 dc

Rnd 2 (dc2, dc2 into next st) 6 times (24)

Rnd 3 dc

Split into three 8st rnds and work each as follows:

Rnds 1–3 dc (3 rnds)

Rnd 4 (dc3, dc2 into next st) twice (10)

Rnds 5–12 dc (8 rnds)

Rnd 13 (dc2tog) 5 times (5)

PART TWO:

Working in cream

Ch12 and sl st to join into a circle

Rnd 1 dc

Rnd 2 (dc2, dc2 into next st) 4 times (16)

Split into two 8 st rnds and work each as follows:

Rnds 1–2 dc (2 rnds)

Rnd 3 (dc3, dc2 into next st) twice (10)

Rnds 4–9 dc (6 rnds)

Rnd 10 (dc2tog) 5 times (5)

MAKING UP

See *Stuffing and Sewing* in the *Technicals* section, and the notes below.

NOTES

Fold beak flat and sew horizontally. Sew the two-prong tail piece beneath the three-prong tail piece. Lightly stuff the thighs.

DORA
the Wood Pigeon

Dora is a loveable and very friendly bird with a habit of falling asleep at inappropriate times throughout the day. Think of her whenever you receive a call from a suspiciously unknown number, and especially one that when you answer there's no one there. Chances are Dora could be quietly snoring into her head-set at the other end of the line. You got off lightly if you caught her on a snooze, because when she's awake she has the most persuasive coo around and you'd have probably found you'd bought extra roof insurance you didn't know you even needed, before you got a chance to hang up.

YOU WILL NEED

Main colour: Steel

Colour two: Silver

Colour three: Stone

See also *You will need* list in *Yarn and Other Materials* section, and *Abbreviations*.

BODY/NECK/HEAD

Work as *standard* starting in silver and changing to steel at rnd 24.

LEGS

Work as *standard PERCHING* but with 6 rnds *TIBIA* and 7 rnds *TARSUS* starting in silver and changing to stone after thigh.

WINGS

Work *standard FLYING* in steel.

BEAK

Working in stone

Ch8 and sl st to join into a circle

Rnds 1–2 dc (2 rnds)

Rnd 3 (dc2, dc2tog) twice (6)

Rnds 4–5 dc (2 rnds)

Rnd 6 (dc2tog) 3 times (3)

TAIL

Working in silver

Ch16 and sl st to join into a circle

Change to steel

Rnds 1–6 dc (6 rnds)

Split to two 8 st rnds and work each as follows:

Rnds 1–4 dc (4 rnds)

Rnd 5 dc7, dc2 into next st (9)

Rnds 6–8 dc (3 rnds)

Rnd 9 dc8, dc2 into next st (10)

Rnds 10–12 dc (3 rnds)

Rnd 13 (dc3, dc2tog) twice (8)

Rnd 14 (dc2, dc2tog) twice (6)

Rnd 15 (dc2tog) 3 times (3)

MAKING UP

See *Stuffing and Sewing* in the *Technicals* section, and the notes below.

NOTES

Fold beak flat and sew horizontally. See *Adding the Beak and Creating Character*. Lightly stuff the thighs. For a slightly more advanced addition to this pattern work rnd 23 in cream and then work half of rnd 24 in green to add detail on the back of the neck before changing to steel.

ERNEST
the Canary

Ernest is one of the best health and safety inspectors in the business. Report writing, investigating and measuring all manner of noise levels, height restrictions and vibrations is his thing. He takes the responsibility for protecting everyone around him very seriously (much to the annoyance of his three sons who sometimes sneak out to the park without their helmets on, to hit each other with sticks). Luckily for them, and all of his friends, co-workers and wife, he has a favourite and very distinctive tune, which he whistles while going about his work, so it's quite easy to quickly cease whatever seemingly dangerous activity you're up to and get your feathers straight in time.

YOU WILL NEED

Main colour: Yellow

Colour two: Oatmeal

See also *You will need* list in *Yarn and Other Materials* section, and *Abbreviations*.

BODY/NECK/HEAD

Work as *standard* in yellow.

LEGS

Work as *standard PERCHING* in yellow changing to oatmeal after thigh.

WINGS

Work as *standard FLYING* in yellow.

BEAK

Working in oatmeal

Ch15 and sl st to join into a circle

Rnd 1 dc

Rnd 2 (dc3, dc2tog) 3 times (12)

Rnd 3 (dc2, dc2tog) 3 times (9)

Rnd 4 dc

Rnd 5 (dc1, dc2tog) 3 times (6)

TAIL

Working in yellow

Ch16 and sl st to join into a circle

Rnds 1–6 dc (6 rnds)

Split into two 8 st rnds and work each as follows:

Rnds 1–4 dc (4 rnds)

Rnd 5 dc7, dc2 into next st (9)

Rnds 6–8 dc (3 rnds)

Rnd 9 dc8, dc2 into next st (10)

Rnds 10–12 dc (3 rnds)

Rnd 13 (dc3, dc2tog) twice (8)

Rnd 14 (dc2, dc2tog) twice (6)

Rnd 15 (dc2tog) 3 times (3)

MAKING UP

See *Stuffing and Sewing* in the *Technicals* section, and the notes below.

NOTES

Lightly stuff the beak and thighs.

HENRY
the Raven

Henry has been endowed with a strut, stature and presence from a bygone era. He has had the privilege of the best education money can buy and now he's applying his intelligence and training to serving his country. He knows his self-assured, purposeful stride will only get stronger as his pride and confidence grow with age and direction, and now he's ready to prove himself. As a chick he dreamt of a tall wall in the middle of nowhere defending good from evil, but he's now ready to accept the reality of what a soldier's life offers him.

YOU WILL NEED

Main colour: Black

Colour two: Steel

See also *You will need* list in *Yarn and Other Materials* section, and *Abbreviations*.

BODY/NECK/HEAD

Work as *standard* in black.

LEGS

Work as *standard PERCHING* but with 6 rnds *TIBIA* and 7 rnds *TARSUS* starting in black and changing to steel after thigh.

WINGS

Work as *standard FLYING* in black.

BEAK

Working in steel

Ch18 and sl st to join into a circle

Rnds 1–4 dc (4 rnds)

Rnd 5 (dc4, dc2tog) 3 times (15)

Rnds 6–8 dc (3 rnds)

Rnd 9 (dc3, dc2tog) 3 times (12)

Rnds 10–11 dc (2 rnds)

Rnd 12 (dc2, dc2tog) 3 times (9)

Rnds 13–14 dc (2 rnds)

Rnd 15 (dc1, dc2tog) 3 times (6)

TAIL

Working in black

Ch16 and sl st to join into a circle

Rnds 1–6 dc (6 rnds)

Split into two 8 st rnds and work each as follows:

Rnds 1–4 dc (4 rnds)

Rnd 5 dc7, dc2 into next st (9)

Rnds 6–8 dc (3 rnds)

Rnd 9 dc8, dc2 into next st (10)

Rnds 10–12 dc (3 rnds)

Rnd 13 (dc3, dc2tog) twice (8)

Rnd 14 (dc2, dc2tog) twice (6)

Rnd 15 (dc2tog) 3 times (3)

MAKING UP

See *Stuffing and Sewing* in the *Technicals* section, and the notes below.

NOTES

Stuff the beak and sew up before sewing into position and lightly stuff the thighs.

VINCE
the Blue-footed Booby

Vince is a bird who struts to his own tune and his garish taste in clothing makes him stand out from the hatch. He fancies himself as a gift to the glittery revolving dance floor, and his strong cologne and fluorescent outfits ensure the hens all know he's there. Pride of place in his nest is a three-foot mirror ball, which he ensures is always dust-free and glinting in the sunlight. It makes for quite a vigorous cleaning routine, but that and his hundreds of other shiny, perfectly polished surfaces, mean he's never short of a chance to admire how he shakes his tail feathers.

YOU WILL NEED

Main colour: Cream

Colour two: Chestnut

Colour three: Blue

See also *You will need* list in *Yarn and Other Materials* section, and *Abbreviations*.

BODY/NECK/HEAD

Work as *standard* in cream.

LEGS

Work as *standard SWIMMING* starting in cream and changing to blue after thigh.

WINGS

Work as *standard FLYING* in chestnut.

BEAK

Working in chestnut

Ch20 and sl st to join into a circle

Rnd 1 dc

Rnd 2 (dc8, dc2tog) twice (18)

Rnd 3 dc

Rnd 4 (dc1, dc2tog) 6 times (12)

Rnd 5 (dc1, dc2tog) 4 times (8)

Rnds 6–13 dc (8 rnds)

Rnd 14 (dc2tog) 4 times (4)

TAIL

Working in cream

Ch16 and sl st to join into a circle

Change to chestnut

Rnds 1–6 dc (6 rnds)

Split into two 8 st rnds and work each as follows:

Rnds 1–4 dc (4 rnds)

Rnd 5 dc7, dc2 into next st (9)

Rnds 6–8 dc (3 rnds)

Rnd 9 dc8, dc2 into next st (10)

Rnds 10–12 dc (3 rnds)

Rnd 13 (dc3, dc2tog) twice (8)

Rnd 14 (dc2, dc2tog) twice (6)

Rnd 15 (dc2tog) 3 times (3)

MAKING UP

See *Stuffing and Sewing* in the *Technicals* section, and the notes below.

NOTES

Stuff the beak and thighs lightly. Lightly stuff the tail at the base and sew the tail in the alert position.

ALAN
the Magpie

Alan is just moving into his golden years and is unsure about adopting a pace of existence with time to reflect. He managed successfully to steer an acclaimed career and a happy family unit through all the sorrows and joys that life throws at you. With his daughter's new-born girl and boy to keep things busy, he might not feel the drop in pace for a while. Although lamenting the move into retirement, it frees him up for some big adventures: more time to discover the secret places in the world he's always been too busy to stop and explore.

YOU WILL NEED

Main colour: Black

Colour two: Cream

Colour three: Green

See also *You will need* list in *Yarn and Other Materials* section, and *Abbreviations*.

BODY/NECK/HEAD

Work as *standard* colour changing from cream to black at rnd 15.

LEGS

Use *standard PERCHING* starting in cream and changing to black after thigh.

WINGS

Work as *standard FLYING* starting in green, working rnds 14–15 in cream and then continuing in black.

BEAK

Working in black

Ch18 and sl st to join into a circle

Rnds 1–4 dc (4 rnds)

Rnd 5 (dc4, dc2tog) 3 times (15)

Rnds 6–8 dc (3 rnds)

Rnd 9 (dc3, dc2tog) 3 times (12)

Rnds 10–11 dc (2 rnds)

Rnd 12 (dc2, dc2tog) 3 times (9)

Rnds 13–14 dc (2 rnds)

Rnd 15 (dc1, dc2tog) 3 times (6)

TAIL

Working in cream

Ch16 and sl st to join into a circle

Change to green

Rnds 1–6 dc (6 rnds)

Split into two 8 st rnds and work each as follows:

Rnds 1–4 dc (4 rnds)

Rnd 5 dc7, dc2 into next st (9)

Rnds 6–8 dc (3 rnds)

Rnd 9 dc8, dc2 into next st (10)

Rnds 10–12 dc (3 rnds)

Rnd 13 (dc3, dc2tog) twice (8)

Rnd 14 (dc2, dc2tog) twice (6)

Rnd 15 (dc2tog) 3 times (3)

MAKING UP

See *Stuffing and Sewing* in the *Technicals* section, and the notes below.

NOTES

For an alternative monochrome magpie simply work all the green parts in black. Stuff the beak and sew up before sewing into position and lightly stuff the thighs.

INA
the Stork

Ina is a midwife who loves new life, tiny feet and the joy that motherhood brings to all the birds she meets. Rather than exhausted, she find she clocks off her twelve-hour shifts exhilarated by her work, and this means that she has had the energy to sample many of the world's most weird and wonderful hobbies over the last twenty years. Despite discovering that she really is very good at fencing, figurine painting and calligraphy (to name but a few) she's settled upon joining her local choir. All things considered, this is an odd choice for a leggy mute bird, so perhaps there's some truth in one little sparrow's stories about her and the handsome choir conductor.

YOU WILL NEED

Main colour: Cream

Colour two: Orange

Colour three: Black

See also *You will need* list in *Yarn and Other Materials* section, and *Abbreviations*.

BODY/NECK/HEAD

Work as *standard* in cream extending neck by 5 rnds.

LEGS

Working in cream

Ch12 and sl st to join into a circle

Rnds 1–3 dc (3 rnds)

Rnd 4 (dc2, dc2tog) 3 times (9)

Rnd 5 (dc1, dc2tog) 3 times (6)

Change colour to orange

Rnds 6–14 dc (9 rnds)

Rnd 15 (dc2 into next st) 6 times (12)

Rnds 16–17 dc (2 rnds)

Rnd 18 (dc2tog) 6 times (6)

Rnds 19–28 dc (10 rnds)

Rnd 29 (dc2 into next st) 6 times (12)

Rnd 30 (dc1, dc2 into next st) 6 times (18)

Split into three 6 st rnds and work each as follows:

DIGITS:

Rnds 1–4 dc (4 rnds)

Rnd 5 dc2tog, dc4 (5)

Rnds 6–7 dc (2 rnds)

Rnd 8 dc2tog, dc3 (4)

Rnd 9 (dc2tog) twice (2)

BACK DIGIT (optional):

Sl st traverse a 6 st root on the back of the foot (see *Adding Details* in *Technicals*) and work as follows:

Rnds 1–2 dc (2 rnds)

Rnd 3 (dc2tog) 3 times (3)

WINGS

Work as *standard FLYING* starting in black and changing to cream at rnd 9.

BEAK

Working in orange

Ch15 and sl st to join into a circle

Rnds 1–3 dc (3 rnds)

Rnd 4 (dc3, dc2tog) 3 times (12)

Rnds 5–7 dc (3 rnds)

Rnd 8 (dc2, dc2tog) 3 times (9)

Rnds 9–11 dc (3 rnds)

Rnd 12 (dc1, dc2tog) 3 times (6)

Rnds 13–14 dc (2 rnds)

Rnd 15 (dc2tog) 3 times (3)

TAIL

Starting in cream

Ch18 and sl st to join into a circle

Rnds 1–3 dc (3 rnds)

Rnd 4 (dc2, dc2 into next st) 6 times (24)

Rnd 5 dc

Split into three 8 st rnds and work each as follows:

Rnds 1–3 dc (3 rnds)

Colour change to black

Rnds 4–7 dc (4 rnds)

Rnd 8 (dc2, dc2tog) twice (6)

Rnd 9 (dc2tog) 3 times (3)

MAKING UP

See *Stuffing and Sewing* in the *Technicals* section, and the notes below.

NOTES

Lightly stuff the beak and thighs.

DUKE
the Mallard

Duke is a duck about town. He is a wild but distinctly urban drake with a slicked-back wet-look comb-over and brightly coloured trousers. Despite his caddish looks he's never short of a new duck to fall for his classic good looks and is always to be found waddling round his local city's parks with his latest sweetheart on his wing. He will read her mediocre love-poetry while they patiently wait for everyone's children to go home, so they can take their turn on the merry-go-round. Then he'll treat her to an ice-cream, and wait for the sun to go down to make his move.

YOU WILL NEED

Main colour: Silver

Colour two: Orange

Colour three: Green

Colour four: Yellow

Colour five: Black

Colour six: Chestnut

Colour seven: Cream

See also *You will need* list in *Yarn and Other Materials* section, and *Abbreviations*.

BODY/NECK/HEAD

Work as *standard* starting in silver with rnds 20–21 in chestnut, rnd 22 in cream and continuing in green.

LEGS

Work as *standard PADDLING* starting in silver and colour changing to orange after thigh.

WINGS

Work as *standard FLYING* in silver.

BEAK

Working in yellow

Begin by dc6 into foundation ring (see *Technicals*)

Rnd 1 (dc2 into next st) 6 times (12)

Rnd 2 (dc1, dc2 into next st) 6 times (18)

Rnds 3–8 dc (6 rnds)

Rnd 9 (dc7, dc2tog) twice (16)

Rnd 10 dc

Rnd 11 (dc7, dc2 into next st) twice (18)

Rnd 12 dc

Rnd 13 (dc5, dc2 into next st) 3 times (21)

TAIL

Starting in silver

Ch12 and sl st to join into a circle

Change to black

Rnds 1–4 dc (4 rnds)

Rnd 5 (dc4, dc2tog) twice (10)

Rnds 6–9 dc (4 rnds)

Rnd 10 (dc3, dc2tog) twice (8)

Rnds 11–12 dc (2 rnds)

Rnd 13 (dc2tog) 4 times (4)

MAKING UP

See *Stuffing and Sewing* in the *Technicals* section, and the notes below.

NOTES

Fold beak flat and sew into position horizontally. Sew the tail into position and then sew upwards from the base through the tip and pull tight before securing to make the shape curl towards the body.

ETHEL
the Kiwi

Ethel has been happily married for thirty years this year. In her time as the perfectly dedicated wife she's worked hard to build up her reputation as the hen that lays the biggest eggs of them all. Her success as a mother she puts down to her time spent honing her phenomenal sense of smell. She follows her beak on what to eat and what to not eat, filling up on only the finest and most nutritious super-seeds she can find until she's overstuffed and fit to burst. Then once she's laid her egg, she defers all responsibility to her dutiful husband, puts her feet up and waits for hatching time.

YOU WILL NEED

Main colour: Fudge

Colour two: Stone

See also *You will need* list in *Yarn and Other Materials* section, and *Abbreviations*.

BODY/NECK/HEAD

Work as *standard* in fudge.

LEGS

Work as *standard PERCHING* starting in fudge and changing to stone after thigh. Don't work the optional claw even if you're an expert (they only have three front facing large toes!).

WINGS

Work as *standard ORNAMENTAL* in fudge.

BEAK

Working in stone

Ch18 and sl st to join into a circle

Rnds 1–4 dc

Rnd 5 (dc4, dc2tog) 3 times (15)

Rnd 6 dc

Rnd 7 (dc2tog) 3 times, dc9 (12)

Rnd 8 dc

Rnd 9 dc10, dc2tog (11)

Rnd 10 dc9, dc2tog (10)

Rnd 11 dc8 dc2tog (9)

Rnds 12–13 dc (2 rnds)

Rnd 14 dc7, dc2tog (8)

Rnd 15 (dc2 dc2tog) twice (6)

Rnds 16–19 dc (4 rnds)

Rnd 20 (dc1, dc2tog) twice (4)

Rnd 21 dc2tog twice (2)

MAKING UP

See *Stuffing and Sewing* in the *Technicals* section, and the notes below.

NOTES

Working in fudge, cover the body and head in ch12 st loops (see *Chain Loops for Feathers* in *Adding Details*) starting from the top of the head and leaving the bottom bare so she sits down. Stuff the beak firmly.

DAVE
the Seagull

Dave has an opportunistic philosophy and a nomadic lifestyle as he's yet to find someone to build a sandcastle for and make an egg with. For breakfast he likes to search the seafront dustbins for any trace of yesterday's forgotten picnic, but to sate his lunchtime appetite he needs to resort to more desperate measures. His favourite food is any kind of potato. When hunger calls he's not afraid to start dive-bombing for fresh salt and vinegary chips straight out of the sandy hands of unwitting children.

YOU WILL NEED

Main colour: Cream

Colour two: Steel

Colour three: Yellow

Colour four: Black

Colour five: Orange

See also *You will need* list in *Yarn and Other Materials* section, and *Abbreviations*.

BODY/NECK/HEAD

Work as *standard* in cream.

LEGS

Work as *standard PADDLING* starting in cream and changing to yellow after the thigh.

WINGS

Work as *standard SOARING* in steel.

BEAK

Working in yellow

Ch12 and sl st to join into a circle

Rnds 1–5 dc (5 rnds)

Rnd 6 (dc4, dc2tog) twice (10)

Rnds 7–8 dc (2 rnds)

Rnd 9 (dc2 into next st) twice, dc8 (12)

Rnds 10–11 dc (2 rnds)

Change to orange

Rnd 12 (dc2tog) 3 times, dc6 (9)

Rnd 13 (dc2tog) 3 times, dc3 (6)

Rnd 14 dc

Rnd 15 (dc2tog) 3 times (3)

TAIL

Working in cream

Ch16 and sl st to join into a circle

Change to black

Rnds 1–6 dc (6 rnds)

Split into two 8 st rnds and work each as follows:

Rnds 1–4 dc (4 rnds)

Rnd 5 dc7, dc2 into next st (9)

Rnds 6–8 dc (3 rnds)

Rnd 9 dc8, dc2 into next st (10)

Rnds 10–12 dc (3 rnds)

Rnd 13 (dc3, dc2tog) twice (8)

Rnd 14 (dc2, dc2tog) twice (6)

Rnd 15 (dc2tog) 3 times (3)

MAKING UP

See *Stuffing and Sewing* in the *Technicals* section, and the notes below.

NOTES

Lightly stuff the beak and thighs.

SOPHIA
the Flamingo

Sophia has not quite grown into her legs yet. This week at school she has had a few tough days when the smaller birds pointed out her knobbly knees, so she's developed a bit of a habit of standing on one leg. Her friends say that the other girls are just jealous, and that picking on Sophia's height distracts from their own worries about their small wings. After a good chat with her mum Sophia drifts off to sleep reassured that one day soon she'll tower over all the other birds with an elegance and femininity befitting her colour.

YOU WILL NEED

Main colour: Pink

Colour two: Black

Colour three: Cream

See also *You will need* list in *Yarn and Other Materials* section, and *Abbreviations*.

BODY/NECK/HEAD

Work as *standard* in pink, extending the neck by 8 rnds.

LEGS

Work as *standard PADDLING* in pink extending *TIBIA* and *TARSUS* to 11 rnds. Work the *CLAWS* in black.

WINGS

Work as *standard FLYING* starting in black and changing to pink at rnd 9.

BEAK

Working in cream

Ch18 and sl st to join into a circle

Rnds 1–4 dc (4 rnds)

Rnd 5 (dc4, dc2tog) 3 times (15)

Rnds 6–8 dc (3 rnds)

Change to black

Rnd 9 (dc2 into next st) 5 times, (dc2tog) 5 times (15)

Rnds 10–11 dc (2 rnds)

Rnd 12 (dc2tog) 6 times, dc 3 (9)

Rnd 13 (dc2tog) 3 times, dc 3 (6)

Rnd 14 dc

Rnd 15 (dc2tog) 3 times (3)

TAIL

Working in pink

Ch18 and sl st to join into a circle

Rnds 1–3 dc (3 rnds)

Rnd 4 (dc2, dc2 into next st) 6 times (24)

Rnd 5 dc

Split into three 8 st rnds and work each as follows:

Rnd 1–7 dc (7 rnds)

Rnd 8 (dc2, dc2tog) twice (6)

Rnd 9 (dc2tog) 3 times (3)

MAKING UP

See *Stuffing and Sewing* in the *Technicals* section, and the notes below.

NOTES

Lightly stuff the beak and thighs.

HUCK
the Pelican

Huck is a fire-fighting hero. In between pole-sliding drills, and of course responding to any actual emergencies, he's become a demon poker player, enthusiastic baker and has a ping-pong back hand that you really wouldn't want to get in the way of. Contrary to what his well-worn apron, drawer of utensils and recipe book collection would suggest, he's actually a very average cook. Rather than lack of skill or effort however, this may just be because, generally halfway though the most vital process in any meal, he's called away to save the day and scoop up more kittens in his beak.

YOU WILL NEED

Main colour: Cream

Colour two: Yellow

Colour three: Black

See also *You will need* list in *Yarn and Other Materials* section, and *Abbreviations*.

BODY/NECK/HEAD

Work as *standard* in cream extending neck by 4 rnds.

LEGS

Work as *standard SWIMMING* starting in cream and changing to yellow after thigh.

WINGS

Work as *SOARING* starting black and changing to cream at rnd 13.

BEAK

Working in yellow

Begin by dc6 into foundation ring (see *Technicals*)

Rnd 1 (dc2 into next st) 6 times (12)

Rnd 2 (dc1, dc2 into next st) 6 times (18)

Rnd 3 (dc2, dc2 into next st) 6 times (24)

Rnds 4-8 dc (5 rnds)

Next:

(dc2 into next, dc1) 4 times and split off the last 10 sts you have worked into a separate round. On these 10 sts:

Rnds 1-10 dc

Rnd 11 (dc3, dc2tog) twice (8)

Rnds 12-14 dc (3 rnds)

Rnd 15 (dc2, dc2tog) twice (6)

TAIL

Working in cream

Ch18 and sl st to join into a circle

Rnds 1-2 dc (2 rnds)

Rnd 3 (dc2, dc2 into next st) 6 times (24)

Rnd 4 dc

Split into three rounds of 8 sts and work each as follows:

Rnds 1-4 dc (4 rnds)

Rnd 5 (dc2tog) 4 times (4)

MAKING UP

See *Stuffing and Sewing* in the *Technicals* section, and the notes below.

NOTES

Sew the beak in position as shown with the option of sewing it closed or leaving it open to fit fish in! Lightly stuff the thighs.

LEVEL 2

Level 2 birds introduce the loop stitch technique and include some patterns that require demanding splitting techniques.

As in Level 1 there is an 'optional' fourth digit, this time on the *GRASPING* feet of the birds of prey. The slip stitch traverse root technique is easier than it sounds, or you can always revisit and add them on retrospectively once you are more confident.

HAZEL
the Hen

Hazel is a frantically industrious red hen. Long since done asking for help from anyone, she's enrolled in every night class going in order to learn to do, well, almost everything. Forget finding someone to assist you in removing some wallpaper, this independent and highly practical hen can change tyres, lay brick walls and has even baked and frosted a five-tier wedding cake. And not only that, she does the lot without the assistance of machines; seriously, this hen won't even take help from her plug-in whisk! After she's sown the corn, harvested and made the flour, the pleasure is in eating a mouthful of her 100 percent fabulous bread.

YOU WILL NEED

Main colour: Fudge

Colour two: Camel

Colour three: Oatmeal

Colour four: Orange

See also *You will need* list in *Yarn and Other Materials* section, and *Abbreviations*.

BODY/NECK/HEAD

Work as *standard* in fudge.

LEGS

Work as *standard PERCHING* but with 6 rnds *TIBIA* and 7 rnds *TARSUS* starting in fudge and changing to oatmeal after thigh.

WINGS

Work as *standard FLAPPING* in camel.

BEAK

Working in oatmeal

Ch8 and sl st to join into circle

Rnds 1–2 dc (2 rnds)

Rnd 3 (dc2, dc2tog) twice (6)

Rnds 4–5 dc (2 rnds)

Rnd 6 (dc1, dc2tog) twice (4)

COMB

Working in orange

Ch18 and sl st to join into circle

Rnd 1 dc

Rnd 2 (dc2, dc2 into next st) 6 times (24)

Split into three 8 sts rnds and work each as follows:

Rnd 1 dc

Rnd 2 (dc2, dc2tog) twice (6)

Rnd 3 dc

Rnd 4 (dc2tog) 3 times (3)

TAIL

Working in camel

Work two lines of four ch20 loops horizontally on the back where you would normally sew the tail. See *Chain Loops for Feathers* in *Adding Details*.

MAKING UP

See *Stuffing and Sewing* in the *Technicals* section, and the notes below.

NOTES

Lightly stuff the comb, beak and thighs.

BARNEY
the Owl

Barney is a number-crunching love-sick owl; a mathematics teacher whose mum is desperately trying her best to mend his broken heart. Lately the look in his shiny mischievous eyes has been replaced with a wide-eyed vacant stare, and as each day goes by he gets a little bit paler and not even his mum's home-cooking can fix it. Until he once again meets that night-loving individual to laugh at him while he calculates the exact angle at which to hunt prey, you can hear his wistful screeching in the last few hours before dawn.

YOU WILL NEED

Main colour: Camel

Colour two: Cream

Colour three: Stone

Colour four: Black

See also *You will need* list in *Yarn and Other Materials* section, and *Abbreviations*.

BODY/NECK/HEAD

Work as *standard* in cream changing to camel at rnd 25.

LEGS

Work as *standard GRASPING* starting in cream and changing to stone at rnd 15. Work *CLAWS* in black.

WINGS

Work as *standard SOARING* in camel.

BEAK (worked flat)

Working in stone

Ch4, turn, dc3 back along ch, turn, dc2 sts back the other way.

EYES

Working in cream

Begin by dc6 into foundation ring (see *Technicals*)

Rnd 1 (dc2 into next st) 6 times (12)

Rnd 2 (dc1, dc2 into next st) 6 times (18)

Rnd 3 dc9 in camel (this is an incomplete rnd)

TAIL

Working in cream

Ch16 and sl st to join into a circle

Rnds 1–2 dc

Rnd 3 (dc1, dc2 into next st) 8 times (24)

Rnds 4–5 dc (2 rnds)

Next split into three 8 sts rnds and work right and left 8 st rnds as follows in camel:

Rnds 6–9 dc (4 rnds)

Rnd 10 dc7, dc2 into next st (9)

Rnd 11 dc

Rnd 12 dc8, dc2 into next st (10)

Rnds 13–15 dc (3 rnds)

Rnd 16 (dc3, dc2tog) 2 times (8)

Rnd 17 (dc2, dc2tog) 2 times (6)

Rnd 18 (dc2tog) 3 times (3)

Work central 8 st rnd as follows:

Rnds 6–9 dc (4 rnds)

Rnd 10 dc7, dc2 into next st (9)

Rnds 11–14 dc (4 rnds)

Rnd 15 dc8, dc2 into next st (10)

Rnds 16–18 dc (3 rnds)

Rnd 19 (dc3, dc2tog) 2 times (8)

Rnd 20 (dc2, dc2tog) 2 times (6)

Rnd 21 (dc2tog) 3 times (3)

MAKING UP

See *Stuffing and Sewing* in the *Technicals* section, and the notes below.

NOTES

Sew the eyes onto the face with camel – half rounds at top and meeting in the middle. Sew the beak in between.

ELIZABETH
the Dodo

There's nothing obsolete about Liz the dodo and her brilliantly organized mind. Peddling a contented happy-go-lucky attitude but remaining unobtrusively ambitious, she'll be planning distinctions not extinction into her diary. At the moment the world lies at her feet, and there's a quiet assuredness about her that says she'll get to wherever she wants to be. Sensibly she heads back to the nest nice and early most nights, combines and reprioritizes her various lists, and then every morning bobs back fresh and ready to reorder the next day.

YOU WILL NEED

Main colour: Steel

Colour two: Oatmeal

Colour three: Cream

Colour four: Camel

Colour five: Black

See also *You will need* list in *Yarn and Other Materials* section, and *Abbreviations*.

BODY/NECK/HEAD

Work as *standard* in steel.

LEGS

Work as *standard GRASPING* starting in steel and changing at rnd 7 to oatmeal. Work *CLAWS* in black.

WINGS

Work as *standard ORNAMENTAL* in cream.

BEAK

Working in oatmeal

Ch24 and sl st to join into circle

Rnds 1–2 dc (2 rnds)

Rnd 3 (dc2, dc2tog) 6 times (18)

Rnd 4 (dc4, dc2tog) 3 times (15)

Rnd 5 (dc3, dc2tog) 3 times (12)

Rnds 6–8 dc (3 rnds)

Rnd 9 (dc2 into next st) 6 times, dc6 (18)

Change to camel

Rnds 10–12 dc (3 rnds)

Rnd 13 (dc2tog) 6 times, dc6 (12)

Rnd 14 (dc2tog) 5 times, dc2 (7)

Rnd 15 dc

Rnd 16 (dc2tog) 3 times, dc1 (4)

TAIL

Work in cream with a loop st every 4th st

Begin by dc6 into foundation ring (see *Technicals*)

Rnd 1 (dc2 into next st) 6 times (12)

Rnd 2 (dc1, dc2 into next st) 6 times (18)

Rnd 3 (dc2, dc2 into next st) 6 times (24)

Rnds 4–7 dc (4 rnds)

MAKING UP

See *Stuffing and Sewing* in the *Technicals* section, and the notes below.

NOTES

Stuff the beak, tail and thighs.

MATEO
the Cock of the Rock

Mateo is an adrenaline junkie on the edge. It all began with a no-responsibility lifestyle and a healthy enjoyment of extreme sports and anything involving a larger than normal amount of danger. But, the thrill he got from bungee jumping, caving and kayaking reduced the more he did it, and the added drama of someone telling him not to disappeared with his last girlfriend. To ensure his next jolt, Mateo seems to be adopting a progressively reckless attitude to his daily life, and driving without his lights on in the middle of the road has become a norm. How far will he go in his increasingly unhinged pursuit of a high heart-rate?

YOU WILL NEED

Main colour: Orange

Colour two: Black

Colout three: Yellow

Colour four: Silver

See also *You will need* list in *Yarn and Other Materials* section, and *Abbreviations*.

BODY/NECK/HEAD

Work as *standard* in orange and work rnds 35–40 with loop st every 4th st.

LEGS

Work as *standard PERCHING* starting in orange and changing to yellow after thigh.

WINGS

Work as *standard FLYING* starting in silver and changing to black at rnd 9.

BEAK

Working in yellow

Ch6 and sl st to join into circle

Rnds 1–3 dc (3 rnds)

Rnd 4 (dc2tog) 3 times (3)

TAIL

Working in orange

Ch 16 and sl st to join into circle

Change to black

Rnds 1–6 dc (6 rnds)

Split into two 8 st rnds and work each as follows:

Rnds 1–4 dc (4 rnds)

Rnd 5 dc7, dc2 into next st (9)

Rnds 6–8 dc (3 rnds)

Rnd 9 dc8, dc2 into next st (10)

Rnds 10–12 dc (3 rnds)

Rnd 13 (dc3, dc2tog) twice (8)

Rnd 14 (dc2, dc2tog) twice (6)

Rnd 15 (dc2tog) 3 times (3)

MAKING UP

See *Stuffing and Sewing* in the *Technicals* section, and the notes below.

NOTES

Fold beak flat and sew on vertically high on the face between the eyes. Lightly stuff the thighs.

EMILY
the Vulture

Emily is not your average young vulture and should not be judged by her hump. Far from a scavenging, unscrupulous loiterer, she is a fast-paced risk-taker who really likes to get things done. Having recently flown the nest, perhaps a little later than some, she's enjoying independent decision making, from how to budget her bills to which leftovers to pack into her lunchbox. Every morning she flies off to her new job with a wave of enthusiasm that keeps her perhaps a little above the speed limit, and lands her ready to tear into the latest day.

YOU WILL NEED

Main colour: Camel

Colour two: Oatmeal

Colour three: Chestnut

Colour four: Cream

Colour five: Black

See also *You will need* list in *Yarn and Other Materials* section, and *Abbreviations*.

BODY/NECK/HEAD

Work as *standard* starting in chestnut and change to work rnd 24 in cream with loop st every 2nd st. Next change to oatmeal and extend neck by 3 rnds before continuing as *standard*.

LEGS

Work as *standard GRASPING* but work rnds 1–2 in cream with loop st every 4th st and then rnds 3–5 in camel before changing to oatmeal to continue as *standard*. Work CLAWS in black.

WINGS

Work as *standard SOARING* in camel.

BEAK

Working in camel

Ch18 and sl st to join into a circle

Rnds 1–2 dc (2 rnds)

Rnd 3 (dc1, dc2tog) 6 times (12)

Rnd 4 dc

Rnd 5 (dc2 into next st) 6 times, dc6 (18)

Rnds 6–9 dc (4 rnds)

Rnd 10 (dc2tog) 6 times, dc6 (12)

Rnd 11 (dc3, dc2tog) twice, dc2 (10)

Rnd 12 dc4, (dc2tog) 3 times (7)

Rnd 13 (dc2tog) twice, (dc2 into next st) twice, dc1. (7)

Sew up to a point.

TAIL

Working in chestnut

Ch18 and sl st to join into a circle

Change to camel

Rnds 1–3 dc (3 rnds)

Rnd 4 (dc2, dc2 into next st) 6 times (24)

Rnd 5 dc

Split into three 8 sts rnds and work each as follows

Rnds 1–7 dc (7 rnds)

Rnd 8 (dc2, dc2tog) twice (6)

Rnd 9 (dc2tog) 3 times (3)

MAKING UP

See *Stuffing and Sewing* in the *Technicals* section, and the notes below.

NOTES

Stuff the top of the wings to act as shoulder pads and sew very high around the neck. Stuff the beak. Cut the loop sts and lightly stuff the thighs.

FLORIAN
the Ostrich

Florian works in fashion. Some say that his career path formed inside his giant egg, as from the moment of hatching he boasted a stronger beak, longer legs and more voluminous plumage than the rest of the flock had ever seen. Twenty-five years of meticulous preening has ensured he has stayed in topnotch condition (a beauty regime which adamantly rejects any 'head in the sand' treatments). Last year he astutely recognized that he had peaked in his modelling career, and is getting ready to become the pride of all who know him when he reveals his own signature collection this spring and strongly strides off the catwalk and onto the shop-floor.

YOU WILL NEED

Main colour: Black

Colour two: Oatmeal

Colour three: Cream

Colour four: Stone

See also *You will need* list in *Yarn and Other Materials* section, and *Abbreviations*.

BODY/NECK/HEAD

Work as *standard* starting in black and changing to oatmeal at rnd 23 and extending neck by 10 rnds.

LEGS

THIGH

Working in black

Ch16 and sl st to join into a circle

Change to oatmeal

Rnds 1–5 dc (5 rnds)

Rnd 6 (dc2, dc2tog) 4 times (12)

Rnd 7 (dc2, dc2tog) 3 times (9)

TIBIA

Rnds 8–13 dc (6 rnds)

ANKLE

Rnd 14 (dc2, dc2 into next st) 3 times (12)

Rnds 15–16 dc (2 rnds)

Rnd 17 (dc1, dc2tog) 4 times (8)

TARSUS

Rnds 18–27 dc (10 rnds)

Rnd 28 (dc1, dc2 into next st) 4 times (12)

FOOT

Split into two 6 st rnds and work each as follows:

Rnds 1–3 dc (3 rnds)

Rnd 4 (dc1, dc2 into next st) 3 times (9)

Rnds 5–8 dc (4 rnds)

Rnd 9 (dc1, dc2tog) 3 times (6)

Rnd 10 dc

Change to black

Rnd 11 dc

Rnd 12 (dc2tog) 3 times (3)

WINGS

Working in black

Use *standard* Work as *standard* HEAD/NECK/BODY up to 30 sts

Rnds 5–6 dc (2 rnds)

Rnd 7 (dc3, dc2tog) 6 times (24)

Split an 8 st rnd and work 'TIP' in cream as follows:

Rnds 1–4 dc (4 rnds)

Rnd 5 (dc2tog) 4 times (4)

Rejoin black yarn and work 3 rnds on 16 sts

Split an 8 sts rnd and work 'TIP' in cream as above

Rejoin black yarn and dc 2 rnds on the final 8 sts then change to cream and work final 'TIP' as above.

BEAK

Working in stone

Begin by dc6 into foundation ring (see *Technicals*)

Rnd 1 (dc2 into next st) 6 times (12)

Rnds 2–7 dc (6 rnds)

Rnd 8 (dc1, dc2 into next st) 3 times, dc6 (15)

Rnd 9 (dc2 into next st, dc2) 3 times, dc6 (18)

Rnd 10 dc

TAIL

Work in cream with a loop st every 4th st

Begin by dc6 into foundation ring (see *Technicals*)

Rnd 1 (dc2 into next st) 6 times (12)

Rnd 2 (dc1, dc2 into next st) 6 times (18)

Rnd 3 (dc2, dc2 into next st) 6 times (24)

Rnds 4–7 dc (4 rnds)

MAKING UP

See *Stuffing and Sewing* in the *Technicals* section, and the notes below.

NOTES

Lightly stuff the beak, tail and thighs.

ROSS
the Turkey

Ross is fed up with his innate ability to make everyone laugh-out-loud getting in the way of his love life. Despite several personality reinvention attempts, he just cannot seem shed the fact that the party follows him wherever he goes, and everyone is too busy having a good time to consider a future date. Most recently he's hatched a plan to renovate his image and meet a mate by joining his local slimming group. If he can resist the temptation to gobble up everyone else's snacks then this time it might just work.

YOU WILL NEED

Main colour: Fudge

Colour two: Chestnut

Colour three: Stone

Colour four: Silver

Colour five: Orange

Colour six: Cream

Colour seven: Black

See also *You will need* list in *Yarn and Other Materials* section, and *Abbreviations*.

BODY/NECK/HEAD

Work as *standard* in chestnut up to rnd 23. Change to orange and work NECK as follows:

Rnd 1 dc

Rnd 2 (dc1, dc2 into next st) 5 times (15)

Rnd 3 dc

Rnd 4 (dc1, dc2tog) 5 times (10)

Rnd 5 dc

Change to silver and continue with HEAD as standard.

LEGS

Work as *standard PERCHING* but with 6 rnds *TIBIA* and 7 rnds *TARSUS* starting in chestnut and changing to stone after thigh.

WINGS

Work as *standard FLAPPING* in fudge.

BEAK

Working in stone

Ch15 and sl st to join into a circle

Rnd 1 dc

Rnd 2 (dc3, dc2tog) 3 times (12)

Rnd 3 dc

Rnd 4 (dc2, dc2tog) 3 times (9)

Rnds 5-6 dc (2 rnds)

Rnd 7 (dc1, dc2tog) 3 times (6)

Rnds 8-10 dc (3 rnds)

Rnd 11 (dc2tog) twice, dc2 (4)

SNOOD (make two)

Working in orange

Begin by dc6 into foundation ring (see *Technicals*)

Ch9 and then sl st back down that chain to ring.

TAIL (worked in two parts)

TOP PLUMAGE

Working in fudge

Ch 18 and sl st to join into a circle

Rnd 1 dc

Rnd 2 (dc2, dc2 into next st) 6 times (24)

Rnd 3 (dc3, dc2 into next st) 6 times (30)

Rnd 4 in chestnut (dc4, dc2 into next st) 6 times (36)

Rnd 5 in fudge (dc5, dc2 into next st) 6 times (42)

Rnd 6 in fudge (dc6, dc2 into next st) 6 times (48)

Split into six 8st rnds and work each as follows:

Rnd 1 in fudge dc

Rnd 2 in chestnut dc

Rnds 3-5 in fudge dc (3 rnds)

Rnd 6 in chestnut dc

Rnds 7-9 in fudge dc (3 rdns)

Rnd 10 in black (dc2, dc2tog) twice (6)

Rnd 11 in cream (dc2tog) 3 times (3)

BOTTOM PLUMAGE

Working in fudge

Ch18 and sl st to join into a circle

Rnd 1 dc

Rnd 2 (dc2, dc2 into next st) 6 times (24)

Split into three 8 st rnds and work each as follows:

Rnds 1-2 in fudge dc (2 rnds)

Rnd 3 in chestnut dc

Rnds 4-6 in fudge dc (3 rnds)

Rnd 7 in chestnut dc

Rnds 8-10 in fudge dc (3 rnds)

Rnd 11 in black (dc2, dc2tog) twice (6)

Rnd 12 in cream (dc2tog) 3 times (3)

MAKING UP

See *Stuffing and Sewing* in the *Technicals* section, and the notes below.

NOTES

Lightly stuff the beak and thighs. Sew the tail in position by gathering ch sts at the bottom of the top plumage and then sewing on the top of the bottom plumage. Sew the 'snood' in position either side of the beak.

KEVIN
the Cassowary

Kevin is a stay at home dad with a very full nest. Every day his wife goes out to work to do whatever it is she does (something important, something boring – he forgets), and he begins the endless housework, school run and laundry routine. Ensuring that everyone has a polished casque before leaving the house is a task in itself, but thankfully he's coached them to sprint the school run in under ten minutes so they are very rarely late. When your feet are as big as cassowary's, four sets of muddy footprints becomes a day-long undertaking to clear up, not to mention ironing all the long socks, shorts and shirts of their incredibly sporty brood.

YOU WILL NEED

Main colour: Black

Colour two: Stone

Colour three: Blue

Colour four: Orange

See also *You will need* list in *Yarn and Other Materials* section, and *Abbreviations*.

BODY/NECK/HEAD

Work as *standard* in black with a loop st every 4th st to rnd 24. Change to orange and extend neck with 3 rnds of orange, and 5 rnds of blue before continuing with *standard* head in blue.

LEGS

Working in black

Ch21 and sl st to join into a circle

Rnds 1–4 dc (4 rnds)

Rnd 5 (dc5, dc2tog) 3 times (18)

Rnds 6–10 dc (5 rnds)

Rnd 11 (dc4, dc2tog) 3 times (15)

Change to stone and work *standard GRASPING* leg without the optional back *DIGIT* (they only have three!). Work *CLAWS* in black.

WINGS

Working in black

In the place where wings would usually be attach three ch16 and sl st back down the chain spines (see *Chain slip sts for feathers* in the *Technicals* section).

BEAK

Working in black

Ch15 and sl st to join into a circle

Rnds 1–3 dc (3 rnds)

Rnd 4 (dc3, dc2tog) 3 times (12)

Rnd 5 (dc2, dc2tog) 3 times (9)

Rnds 6–8 dc (3 rnds)

Rnd 9 (dc1, dc2tog) 3 times (6)

Rnd 10 dc

Rnd 11 (dc2tog) 3 times (3)

CASQUE

Working in stone

Begin by dc6 into foundation ring (see *Technicals*)

Rnd 1 (dc2 into next st) 6 times (12)

Rnd 2 (dc1, dc2 into next st) 6 times (18)

Rnd 3 dc

Rnd 4 (dc2, dc2 into next st) 6 times (24)

Rnd 5–10 dc (6 rnds)

WATTLE (make two)

Working in orange

Begin by dc6 into foundation ring (see *Technicals*) and then ch8.

TAIL

Work in black with a loop st every 4th st

Begin by dc6 into foundation ring (see *Technicals*)

Rnd 1 (dc2 into next st) 6 times (12)

Rnd 2 (dc1, dc2 into next st) 6 times (18)

Rnd 3 (dc2, dc2 into next st) 6 times (24)

Rnds 4–7 dc (4 rnds)

MAKING UP

See *Stuffing and Sewing* in the *Technicals* section, and the notes below.

NOTES

Stuff the casque, beak, thighs and tail. Sew the tail flat before sewing on, sew the stuffed casque open-bottomed onto the top of the head. Sew the wattle onto the three orange rnds on the neck.

TRICIA
the Silkie Chicken

Tricia is a middle-aged, self-employed aerobics instructor thrilled that so many women are still so bad at getting fit and staying thin. Her 'modern pop workout' hasn't been updated since the 80s; it worked for her and her lycra bodysuit then, and if her toy-boy and dress-size are anything to go by, then it's still working now. She's never really been seen without her mullet, sweatband and legwarmers, and if the right Madonna track comes on when she's in the supermarket, then her muscles just move on their own. She's not one for counting her eggs though, because every time the latest spinning, plating or pilates craze takes a hold her attendance numbers take a hit as everyone heads for the next easy-fix solution to cellulite.

YOU WILL NEED

Main colour: Silver

Colour two: Black

See also *You will need* list in *Yarn and Other Materials* section, and *Abbreviations*.

BODY/NECK/HEAD

Work as *standard* in silver up to rnd 24 then continue working a loop st every 4th st.

LEGS

Work as *standard PERCHING* but with 6 rnds *TIBIA* and 7 rnds *TARSUS* in silver with loop st every 4th st on thigh and then change to black to continue but working rnd 25 in silver with loop st every 2nd st.

WINGS

Work as *standard FLAPPING* in silver with loop st every 4th st throughout.

BEAK

Working in black

Ch12 and sl st to join into a circle

Rnd 1 dc

Rnd 2 (dc4, dc2tog) twice (10)

Rnd 3 (dc3, dc2tog) twice (8)

Rnd 4 (dc2, dc2tog) twice (6)

Rnd 5 (dc2tog) twice, (dc2 into next st) twice (6)

Rnd 6 (dc2tog) twice, dc2 (4)

TAIL

Working in silver with a loop st every 4th st

Begin by dc6 into foundation ring (see *Technicals*)

Rnd 1 (dc2 into next st) 6 times (12)

Rnd 2 (dc1, dc2 into next st) 6 times (18)

Rnd 3 (dc2, dc2 into next st) 6 times (24)

Rnds 4-7 dc (4 rnds)

MAKING UP

See *Stuffing and Sewing* in the *Technicals* section, and the notes below.

NOTES

Cut the loops, stuff the beak and tail.

ABRAHAM
the Bald Eagle

All-American Abraham loves big cars and fishing trips. He's an optimistic hardworking bird who's everyone's best friend, and nothing upsets him more than meeting someone having a bad day. Since he graduated high school he's been steadily pursuing his lifestyle, and so far he's living the dream his mom had always hoped for him. He thinks there's nothing better than snatching an unplanned weekend away with his family, bundling the essentials into his gigantic truck and hitting the highway with a belly full of fish to look forward to.

YOU WILL NEED

Main colour: Chestnut

Colour two: Cream

Colour three: Yellow

Colour four: Black

See also *You will need* list in *Yarn and Other Materials* section, and *Abbreviations*.

BODY/NECK/HEAD

Work as *standard* starting in chestnut and working rnd 23 in cream with a loop st every 2nd st and then continuing as *standard* in cream.

LEGS

Work as *standard GRASPING* starting with chestnut and working rnds 1–4 with loop st every 4th st and then changing to yellow. Work *CLAWS* in black.

WINGS

Work as *standard SOARING* in chestnut.

BEAK

Working in yellow

Ch16 and sl st to join into a circle

Rnds 1–4 dc (4 rnds)

Rnd 5 dc4, (dc2tog) 6 times (10)

Rnd 6 (dc2 into next st) 5 times, dc5 (15)

Rnd 7 dc11, (dc2tog) twice (13)

Rnd 8 (dc2tog) twice, dc5, (dc2tog) twice (9)

Rnd 9 dc3 (dc3 into next st) twice, dc4 (13)

Finish by oversewing down the beak from the top to finish at the point.

TAIL

Working in chestnut

Ch18 and sl st to join into a circle

Change to cream

Rnds 1–3 dc (3 rnds)

Rnd 4 (dc2, dc2 into next st) 6 times (24)

Rnd 5 dc

Split into three 8 sts rnds and work each as follows:

Rnds 1–7 dc (7 rnds)

Rnd 8 (dc2, dc2tog) twice (6)

Rnd 9 (dc2tog) 3 times (3)

MAKING UP

See *Stuffing and Sewing* in the *Technicals* section, and the notes below.

NOTES

Cut the loops on the legs and neck. Stuff the beak.

KIT
the Rooster

Kit is an early bird who is always first in the coffee queue (sometimes while the staff are still larking around tying their aprons on). He proudly takes his single-origin, micro-roasted coffee black, and will gladly extol the virtues of every sharp, creamy and earthy note of his experience. Most days he then launches into offering advice to one and all in the coffee shop about their order, how to savour it and how best to express the joy they should feel when taking their morning hit of caffeine. All in all, he's the kind of cock even the most patient and dedicated barista wishes would choke on his cornflakes and not make it to the next dawn.

YOU WILL NEED

Main colour: Camel

Colour two: Green

Colour three: Chestnut

Colour four: Fudge

Colour five: Stone

Colour six: Orange

Colour seven: Oatmeal

See also *You will need* list in *Yarn and Other Materials* section, and *Abbreviations*.

BODY/NECK/HEAD

Work as *standard* starting in green and changing to fudge at rnd 7 and then to camel at rnd 15.

LEGS

Work as *standard PERCHING* starting in camel and changing to stone after thigh.

WINGS

Work as *standard FLAPPING* in chestnut.

BEAK

Working in oatmeal

Ch12 and sl st to join into a circle

Rnd 1 dc

Rnd 2 (dc4, dc2tog) twice (10)

Rnd 3 dc

Rnd 4 (dc3, dc2tog) twice (8)

Rnd 5 dc

Rnd 6 (dc2, dc2tog) twice (6)

Rnd 7 (dc1, dc2tog) twice (4)

Rnd 8 dc

WATTLE (make two)

Working in orange

Begin by dc6 into foundation ring (see *Technicals*)

Rnd 1 (dc2 into next st) 6 times (12)

Rnds 2–3 dc (2 rnds)

Rnd 4 (dc2, dc2tog) 3 times (9)

Rnd 5 dc

Rnd 6 (dc1, dc2tog) 3 times (6)

Rnds 7–8 dc (2 rnds)

Rnd 9 (dc1, dc2 into next st) 3 times (9)

COMB

Working in orange

Ch24 and sl st to join into a circle

Rnd 1 dc

Rnd 2 (dc3, dc2 into next st) 6 times (30)

Rnd 3 dc12, (dc2 into next st) 3 times, dc12, (dc2 into next st) 3 times (36)

Split off 9 sts and work as follows:

Rnd 1 (dc2 into next st) 3 times, dc4 (dc2 into next st) twice (14)

Rnd 2 dc

Rnd 3 (dc2tog) seven times (7)

Rnd 4 (dc2tog) 3 times, dc1 (4)

Rnd 5 (dc2tog) twice (2)

Rejoin yarn and split off next 6 sts and work as follows

Rnds 1–2 dc (2 rnds)

Rnd 3 (dc1, dc2tog) twice (4)

Rnd 4 dc

Rnd 5 (dc2tog) twice (2)

Rejoin yarn and repeat two more 6st rnds, then rejoin yarn to remaining 9 sts and work a 9 st rnd as the first.

TAIL

Working in green

At the point where tail is usually sewn on work two rows of ch20, and ch12 alternate sl st spines (see *Chain slip sts for feathers* in the *Technicals* section). Make around a dozen in total.

MAKING UP

See *Stuffing and Sewing* in the *Technicals* section, and the notes below.

NOTES

Stuff the comb in two end prongs, the beak and thighs.

MARGOT
the Swan

Margot the swan is one of those unforgettable ladies that all young women should meet. With an ethereal sense of her own style that instantly makes everyone else look scruffy, dated and unoriginal, Margot exudes a quality that, if you get close to her, you know might make what happens next change your mind about everything. If you take her fancy she may well stop to speak to you, often with a perfect one-liner of wit, or a question that works on fifteen levels, followed by a swoop of the chin and a piercing snatch of eye contact. As you fluster around for a response she turns and moves on, and leaves you feeling awkward and confused but oddly reassured that you were the one she chose to encounter.

YOU WILL NEED

Main colour: Cream

Colour two: Black

Colour three: Orange

See also *You will need* list in *Yarn and Other Materials* section, and *Abbreviations*.

BODY/NECK/HEAD

Work as *standard* in cream extending neck by 6 rnds.

LEGS

Work as *standard PADDLING* starting in cream and changing to black after thigh.

WINGS

Working in cream

Work as *standard HEAD/NECK/BODY* until

Rnd 4 (dc3, dc2 into next st) 6 times (30)

Rnds 5–10 dc (6 rnds)

Split 10 sts into a rnd and work as follows:

Rnds 1–4 dc (4 rnds)

Rnd 5 (dc2tog) 5 times (5)

Rejoin yarn to remaining 20 sts and dc 3 rnds

Dc5 and split another 10 sts into a rnd and work as follows:

Rnds 1–4 dc (4 rnds)

Rnd 5 (dc2tog) 5 times (5)

Rejoin yarn to remaining 10 sts and work as follows:

Rnds 1–6 dc (6 rnds)

Rnd 7 (dc2tog) 5 times (5)

BEAK

Starting in black

Begin by dc6 into foundation ring (see *Technicals*)

Change to orange

Rnd 1 (dc2 into next st) 6 times (12)

Rnd 2 (dc1, dc2 into next st) 6 times (18)

Rnds 3–5 dc (3 rnds)

Rnd 6 (dc4, dc2tog) 3 times (15)

Rnds 7–12 dc (6 rnds)

Change to black

Rnd 13 (dc3 into next st) 3 times in black, dc11 in orange, dc1 in black (21)

Continue in black

Rnd 14 dc (21)

Rnd 15 (dc2tog) 4 times, dc13 (17)

Rnd 16 (dc1, dc2 into next st) 8 times, dc1 (25)

TAIL

Working in cream

Ch18 and sl st to join into a circle

Rnd 1 dc

Rnd 2 (dc2, dc2 into next st) 6 times (24)

Rnd 3 (dc5, dc2 into next st) 4 times (28)

Split into three rnds with one 12st rnd in the middle and two 8 st rnds either side

On the 8 st rnds work as follows:

Rnds 1–2 dc (2 rnds)

Rnd 3 (dc2tog) 4 times (4)

On the central 12 sts:

Rnds 1–4 dc (4 rnds)

Rnd 5 (dc2, dc2tog) 3 times (9)

Rnd 6 (dc1, dc2tog) 3 times (6)

Rnd 7 (dc2tog) 3 times (3)

MAKING UP

See *Stuffing and Sewing* in the *Technicals* section, and the notes below.

NOTES

Lightly stuff the beak and the thighs and sew wings high on the back.

LEVEL 3

The birds in this section introduce colour changing that requires a certain level of accuracy and discipline because you will need to count a shape pattern and a colour pattern simultaneously. Should you have one more or one less stitch than you ought, or if you misplace or miscount your row starts, you will find that the colour patterns will skew and this will be hard to fix.

When working colour changes that require you to return to the original after less than five stitches, run the strands behind the back of the WS, being careful not to pull the changes too tight to avoid puckering the fabric. Many of the Level 3 birds have the 'climbing leg' standard form, which the less experienced may find a bit challenging (see *Technicals* section).

ELVIS
the Cockatoo

Elvis is a karaoke king with a raucous voice only his late mother loved to hear. The dawn chorus is a terrifying prospect for anyone within earshot of this squawking parrot, especially when he's pulled an all-nighter and has ignored the sundown, having bumbled from branch to branch with his renditions of the old classics. He is a late riser, letting the sun warm the stage before he hops upon it; perhaps that's the key to his longevity as some say he'll have seen a century by this time next year.

YOU WILL NEED

Main colour: Cream

Colour two: Black

Colour three: Yellow

See also *You will need* list in *Yarn and Other Materials* section, and *Abbreviations*.

BODY/NECK/HEAD

Work as *standard* in cream.

LEGS

Work as *standard CLIMBING* starting in cream and changing to black at rnd 9.

WINGS

Work as *standard FLYING* in cream.

BEAK

Working in black

Ch12 and sl st to join into a circle

Rnd 1 dc

Rnd 2 (dc4, dc2tog) twice (10)

Rnd 3 (dc3, dc2tog) twice (8)

Rnd 4 (dc2, dc2tog) twice (6)

Rnd 5 (dc2tog) twice, (dc2 into next st) twice (6)

Rnd 6 (dc2tog) twice, dc2 (4)

CREST

Working in yellow

Ch32 and sl st to join into a circle

Rnds 1–2 dc (2 rnds)

Split into four 8 st rnds and work first 8 st rnd as follows:

Rnds 1–6 dc (6 rnds)

Rnd 7 (dc2, dc2tog) twice (6)

Rnds 8–11 dc (4 rnds)

Rnd 12 (dc1, dc2tog) twice (4)

Rejoin yarn and split off next 8 st rnd and work as follows:

Rnds 1–6 dc (6 rnds)

Rnd 7 (dc2, dc2tog) twice (6)

Rnds 8–13 dc (6 rnds)

Rnd 14 (dc1, dc2tog) twice (4)

Rejoin yarn and split off next 8 sts and repeat first 8 st rnd

Rejoin and work last 8 st rnd as follows:

Rnds 1–4 dc (4 rnds)

Rnd 5 (dc2, dc2tog) twice (6)

Rnd 6 dc

Rnd 7 (dc1, dc2tog) twice (4)

TAIL

Working in cream

Ch18 and sl st to join into a circle

Rnds 1–3 dc (3 rnds)

Rnd 4 (dc2, dc2 into next st) 6 times (24)

Rnd 5 dc

Split into three 8 st rnds and work each as follows:

Rnds 1–7 dc (7 rnds)

Rnd 8 (dc2, dc2tog) twice (6)

Rnd 9 (dc2tog) 3 times (3)

MAKING UP

See *Stuffing and Sewing* in the *Technicals* section, and the notes below.

NOTES

Stuff the crest, beak and thighs.

SCOTT
the Woodpecker

Scott truly believes that he will one day change the world. He is the kind of bird who will peck holes in your roof and then warn you about the dangers of said holes when it rains. Sometimes anti-social, but often overly attentive, he flits between personalities in a way that gives those that love him plenty to mock him for. That said, if you've got a big enough beak to swallow all his life advice then there's a very interesting bird hiding behind that big fuzzy crest, and one day soon he'll stumble across his real chance to fly.

YOU WILL NEED

Main colour: Black

Colour two: Steel

Colour three: Cream

Colour four: Orange

See also *You will need* list in *Yarn and Other Materials* section, and *Abbreviations*.

BODY/NECK/HEAD

Work as *standard* in black and change to cream at rnd 33.

LEGS

Work as *standard CLIMBING* starting in black and changing to steel after rnd 9.

WINGS

Work as *standard FLYING* with rnds 1–5 in cream, rnds 6–20 in black, rnd 21 in cream and then continue to end in black.

BEAK

Working in cream

Ch12 and sl st to join into a circle

Rnds 1–6 dc (6 rnds)

Rnd 7 (dc2, dc2tog) 3 times (9)

Rnds 8–9 dc (2 rnds)

Rnd 10 (dc1, dc2tog) 3 times (6)

Rnds 11–12 dc (2 rnds)

CREST

Working in orange

Ch 30 and sl st to join into a circle

Rnds 1–2 dc (2 rnds)

Rnd 3 (dc2tog) 6 times, dc18 (24)

Rnd 4 (dc10, dc2tog) twice (22)

Rnd 5 (dc9, dc2tog) twice (20)

Rnd 6 (dc8, dc2tog) twice (18)

Rnd 7 (dc4, dc2tog) 3 times (15)

Rnd 8 (dc2tog) 3 times, dc9 (12)

Rnd 9 (dc2tog) twice, dc8 (10)

Rnd 10 dc

Rnd 11 (dc2tog) 5 times (5)

Rnd 12 (dc2tog) twice, dc1 (3)

TAIL

Working in black

Ch16 and sl st to join into a circle

Rnds 1–6 dc (6 rnds)

Split into two 8 st rnds and work each as follows:

Rnds 1–4 dc (4 rnds)

Rnd 5 dc7, dc2 into next st (9)

Rnds 6–8 dc (3 rnds)

Rnd 9 dc8, dc2 into next st (10)

Rnds 10–12 dc (3 rnds)

Rnd 13 (dc3, dc2tog) twice (8)

Rnd 14 (dc2, dc2tog) twice (6)

Rnd 15 (dc2tog) 3 times (3)

MAKING UP

See *Stuffing and Sewing* in the *Technicals* section, and the notes below.

NOTES

Stuff the crest, beak and thighs.

GIANNI
the Lovebird

Gianni loves birds. He loves watching birds, talking to birds and especially dancing with other birds, well the three things are inextricably linked, really. When he sees another bird he just has to talk to them, and once he talks to them he gets a little carried away. You see, when Gianni chats he gestures with his entire body from his eyes to his claws, and the more engaging the conversation the more his shoulders move, and wings flap, until eventually he's dancing without even realizing (and all that was just over ordering some pasta from the waitress).

YOU WILL NEED

Main colour: Lime

Colour two: Silver

Colour three: Orange

Colour four: Yellow

See also *You will need* list in *Yarn and Other Materials* section, and *Abbreviations*.

BODY/NECK/HEAD

Work as *standard* starting in lime, colour changing to yellow at rnd 17 and changing to orange at rnd 22.

LEGS

Work as *standard CLIMBING* starting in lime and changing to silver after rnd 9.

WINGS

Work as *standard FLYING* in lime.

BEAK

Working in silver

Ch12 and sl st to join into a circle

Rnd 1 dc

Rnd 2 (dc4, dc2tog) twice (10)

Rnd 3 (dc3, dc2tog) twice (8)

Rnd 4 (dc2, dc2tog) twice (6)

Rnd 5 (dc2tog) twice, (dc2 into next st) twice (6)

Rnd 6 (dc2tog) twice, dc2 (4)

TAIL

Working in lime

Ch18 and sl st to join into a circle

Rnds 1–3 dc (3 rnds)

Rnd 4 (dc2, dc2 into next st) 6 times (24)

Rnd 5 dc

Split into three 8 st rnds and work each as follows:

Rnds 1–7 dc (7 rnds)

Rnd 8 (dc2, dc2tog) twice (6)

Rnd 9 (dc2tog) 3 times (3)

MAKING UP

See *Stuffing and Sewing* in the *Technicals* section, and the notes below.

NOTES

Lightly stuff the beak and thighs.

MEGHAN
the Toucan

Meghan is a little girl growing an attitude to match her beak. Like many very young women, her attention span is short for anything and everything other than princesses, fairies and the colour pink. What initially began as an interest in happy endings developed into some days when she is insistent about eating food fit only for a queen, and wearing her plastic high heels to nursery. When she's not sitting on the side of her bed, reading about a castle and kicking her feet back and forth, she can be found cruising around on her bike with her tiara on and glitzy streamers fluttering beside her from the bicycle handlebars.

YOU WILL NEED

Main colour: Black

Colour two: Steel

Colour three: Orange

Colour four: Yellow

Colour five: Cream

See also *You will need* list in *Yarn and Other Materials* section, and *Abbreviations*.

BODY/NECK/HEAD

Work as *standard* in black until rnd 21

Rnd 22 (dc2tog) 9 times cream, dc6 black (15)

Rnd 23 (dc2tog) 5 times cream, dc5 black (10)

Rnd 24 dc5 cream, dc5 black

Rnd 25 (dc2 into next st) 5 times cream, (dc2 into next st) 5 times black (20)

Rnd 26 (dc3, dc2 into next st) twice, dc2 cream, dc1, dc2 into next st, (dc3, dc2 into next st) twice black (25)

Rnd 27 (dc4, dc2 into next st) twice, dc2 cream, dc2, dc2 into next st, (dc4, dc2 into next st) twice black (30)

Rnd 28 (dc2, dc2 into next st) 4 times, dc2 cream, dc2 into next st, (dc2, dc2 into next st) 5 times black (40)

Rnds 29-31 dc18 cream, dc22 black (3 rnds)

Rnd 32 dc8, dc2tog, dc8 cream, dc2tog, (dc8, dc2tog) twice black (36)

Rnd 33 dc 17 cream, dc 19 black

Rnd 34 (dc4, dc2tog) twice, dc4 cream, dc2tog across both colours, (dc4, dc2tog) 3 times black (30)

Continue as *standard* in black

LEGS

Work as *standard CLIMBING* starting in black and changing to steel at rnd 9.

WINGS

Work as *standard FLYING* in black.

BEAK

Working in black

Ch24 and sl st to join into a circle

Rnd 1 dc

Change to yellow

Rnds 2-9 dc (8 rnds)

Rnd 10 (dc4, dc2tog) 4 times (20)

Change to orange

Rnds 11-16 dc (6 rnds)

Rnd 17 dc16, (dc2tog) twice (18)

Rnd 18 dc

Rnd 19 dc6, (dc2tog) 3 times, dc6 (15)

Rnd 20 dc8, (dc2tog) 3 times, dc1 (12)

Change to black

Rnd 21 dc8, (dc2tog) twice (10)

Rnd 22 dc6 (dc2tog) twice (8)

Rnd 23 dc2tog, dc4, dc2tog (6)

Rnd 24 dc2tog, dc2, dc2tog (4)

TAIL

Working in black

Ch16 and sl st to join into a circle

Rnds 1-6 dc (6 rnds)

Split to two 8 st rnds and work each as follows:

Rnds 1-4 dc (4 rnds)

Rnd 5 dc7, dc2 into next st (9)

Rnds 6-8 dc (3 rnds)

Rnd 9 dc8, dc2 into next st (10)

Rnds 10-12 dc (3 rnds)

Rnd 13 (dc3, dc2tog) twice (8)

Rnd 14 (dc2, dc2tog) twice (6)

Rnd 15 (dc2tog) 3 times (3)

MAKING UP

See *Stuffing and Sewing* in the *Technicals* section, and the notes below.

NOTES

Stuff the beak firmly. Stuff the thighs lightly.

ROBIN
the Robin

Robin is more than a little obsessed with his wood-burning stove. All summer he sits on his sofa longing for the temperature to drop low enough so that he can start setting light to his carefully arranged log pile. His wife is starting to get concerned that his self-hewn kindling fixation might have gone too far, especially now he's showing an interest in ripping out the cooker. A quick check on his search history online reveals he has plans for a 'build your own' brick oven in the kitchen. Fortunately for all involved, his wife's favourite foods are best served on a crispy crust, so she might as well just buy him a new axe and start practising her kneading. Who knew robins ate pizza?

YOU WILL NEED

Main colour: Stone

Colour two: Cream

Colour three: Orange

Colour four: Chestnut

See also *You will need* list in *Yarn and Other Materials* section, and *Abbreviations*.

BODY/NECK/HEAD

Work as *standard* in cream until

Rnd 16 dc3 orange, dc12 cream, dc15 orange

Rnd 17–18 dc4 orange, dc11 cream, dc15 orange (2 rnds)

Rnd 19 dc5 orange, dc10 cream, dc15 orange

Rnd 20 dc3, dc2tog orange, (dc3, dc2tog) twice cream, (dc3, dc2tog) 3 times orange

Rnd 21 dc5 orange, dc7 stone, dc12 orange

Next dc6 in orange. Move st marker to this point and RESET.

Rnd 22 dc6 stone, (dc2tog) 9 times orange (15)

Rnd 23 dc2tog, dc4 stone, (dc2tog) 4 times, dc1 orange (10)

Rnd 24 dc 5 stone, dc 5 orange

Next dc5 in stone. Move st marker to this point and RESET.

Rnd 25 (dc2 into next st) 5 times orange, (dc2 into next st) 5 times stone (20)

Rnd 26 (dc3, dc2 into next) twice, dc2 orange, dc1, dc2 into next st, (dc3, dc2 into next) twice stone (25)

Rnd 27 (dc4, dc2 into next) twice, dc2 orange, dc2, dc2 into next st, (dc4, dc2 into next) twice stone (30)

Rnd 28 (dc2, dc2 into next) 4 times, dc2 orange, dc2 into next st, (dc2, dc2 into next) 5 times stone (40)

Rnds 29–31 dc18 orange, dc22 stone (3 rnds)

Rnd 32 dc8, dc2tog, dc8 orange, dc2tog, (dc8, dc2tog) twice stone (36)

Rnd 33 dc17 orange, dc19 stone

Rnd 34 (dc4, dc2tog) twice, dc4 orange, dc2tog across both colours, (dc4, dc2tog) 3 times stone (30)

Continue as *standard* in stone.

LEGS

Work as *standard PERCHING* starting with cream and changing to stone after thigh.

WINGS

Work as *standard FLYING* in stone.

BEAK

Working in chestnut

Ch8 and sl st to join in a circle

Rnd 1 dc

Rnd 2 (dc2, dc2tog) twice (6)

Rnds 3–4 dc (2 rnds)

Rnd 5 (dc1, dc2tog) twice (4)

Rnd 6 (dc2tog) twice (2)

TAIL

Working in cream

Ch16 and sl st to join into a circle

Change to stone

Rnds 1–6 dc (6 rnds)

Split to two 8 st rnds and work each as follows:

Rnds 1–4 dc (4 rnds)

Rnd 5 dc7, dc2 into next (9)

Rnds 6–8 dc (3 rnds)

Rnd 9 dc8, dc2 into next (10)

Rnds 10–12 dc (3 rnds)

Rnd 13 (dc3, dc2tog) twice (8)

Rnd 14 (dc2, dc2tog) twice (6)

Rnd 15 (dc2tog) 3 times (3)

MAKING UP

See *Stuffing and Sewing* in the *Technicals* section, and the notes below.

NOTES

Stuff the thighs lightly. Fold beak flat and sew it on vertically.

GARETH
the Puffin

Gareth was caught unawares when he found himself expecting his first puffling when he had barely stopped being one himself. He decided to face the challenge and dived head first into this unchartered territory. Fom being a rebellious boy with a brightly coloured beak, he's now a man who can proudly puff out his chest as he takes his son to swimming lessons.

YOU WILL NEED

Main colour: Cream

Colour two: Black

Colour three: Orange

Colour four: Yellow

See also *You will need* list in *Yarn and Other Materials* section, and *Abbreviations*.

BODY/NECK/HEAD

Starting in cream work as *standard* until

Rnd 6 (dc5, dc2 into next st) 6 times (42)

Rnds 7-8 dc21 black, dc21 cream (2 rnds)

Rnd 9 dc1 cream, dc 20 black, dc 21 cream

Rnd 10 dc1 cream, dc4, dc2tog, (dc5, dc2tog) twice black, (dc5, dc2tog) 3 times cream (36)

Rnds 11-13 dc2 cream, dc16 black, dc18 cream (3 rnds)

Rnd 14 dc3 cream, dc15 black, dc18 cream

Rnd 15 dc3 cream, dc1, dc2tog, (dc4, dc2tog) twice black, (dc4, dc2tog) 3 times cream (30)

Rnd 16 dc3 cream, dc12 black, dc15 cream

Rnds 17-18 dc4 cream, dc11 black, dc15 cream (2 rnds)

Rnd 19 dc5 cream, dc10 black, dc15 cream

Rnd 20 dc3, dc2tog cream, (dc3, dc2tog) twice black, (dc3, dc2tog) three times cream (24)

Rnd 21 dc5 cream, dc7 black, dc12 cream

Then, dc6 cream, dc6 black. Move st marker to this point and RESET

Rnd 22 (dc2tog) 9 times cream, dc2, dc2tog, dc2 black (14)

Rnd 23 (dc1, dc2tog) 3 times cream, dc1, dc2tog, dc2 black (10)

Rnd 24 dc6 cream, dc4 black (10)

Rnd 25 (dc2 into next st) 7 times cream, (dc2 into next st) 3 times black (20)

Rnd 26 (dc3, dc2 into next st) 3 times, dc2 cream, dc1, dc2 into next st, dc3, dc2 into next st (25)

Rnd 27 (dc4, dc2 into next st) 3 times, dc3 cream, dc2 into next st, dc4, dc2 into next st, dc1 black (30)

Rnd 28 (dc2, dc2 into next st) 7 times cream, (dc2, dc2 into next st) 3 times black (40)

Rnd 29 dc28 cream, dc12 black

Rnds 30-31 dc29 cream, dc11 black (2 rnds)

Rnd 32 dc1 black, (dc7, dc2tog) 3 times, dc2 cream, dc6, dc2tog, dc2 black (36)

Rnd 33 dc1 black, dc26 cream, dc9 black

Rnd 34 dc2 black, dc2, dc2tog (dc4, dc2tog) 3 times, dc3 cream, dc1, dc2tog, dc4, dc2tog black (30)

Continue as *standard* in black.

LEGS

Work as *standard SWIMMING* but with 4 rnds *TIBIA* and 6 rnds *TARSUS* starting cream and colour changing to orange after thigh. Work *CLAWS* in black.

WINGS

Work as *standard FLYING* in black.

BEAK

Working in yellow

Ch18 and sl st to join into a circle

Rnd 1 dc in yellow

Rnds 2-3 dc in black (2 rnds)

Rnd 4 (dc 7, dc2tog) twice in yellow (16)

Continue in orange

Rnds 5-6 dc (2 rnds)

Rnd 7 (dc2, dc2tog) 4 times (12)

Rnd 8 (dc1, dc2tog) 4 times (8)

Rnd 9 dc

Rnd 10 (dc2tog) 4 times (4)

Rnd 11 (dc2tog) twice (2)

TAIL

Working in black

Ch18 and sl st to join into a circle

Rnds 1-2 dc (2 rnds)

Rnd 3 (dc2, dc2 into next st) 6 times (24)

Rnd 4 dc

Split into three 8 st rnds and work each as follows:

Rnds 1-4 dc (4 rnds)

Rnd 5 (dc2tog) 4 times (4)

MAKING UP

See *Stuffing and Sewing* in the *Technicals* section, and the notes below.

NOTES

Align and sew on the wings to the body colour changing. Sew tail on the colour change round on bottom of the body. Stuff the beak and lightly stuff the thighs.

ROHIT
the Peacock

Rohit has only just broken the habit of looking over his shoulder to see how long his tail has grown that day. His personal challenge is to cultivate a character big enough to match his plumage. Despite being scared of flying he's taking his first trip abroad this year to meet new people, eat new things and try out the power of his enormous train. His only concern is getting far enough away so that the all-seeing eyes of his mother aren't still peering over his shoulder.

YOU WILL NEED

Main colour: Green

Colour two: Blue

Colour three: Stone

Colour four: Cream

Colour five: Black

Colour six: Camel

See also *You will need* list in *Yarn and Other Materials* section, and *Abbreviations*.

BODY/NECK/HEAD

Work as *standard* in blue extending neck by 3 rnds.

LEGS

Working in blue

Ch12 and sl st to join into a circle

Rnds 1–3 dc (3 rnds)

Rnd 4 (dc2, dc2tog) 3 times (9)

Rnd 5 (dc1, dc2tog) 3 times (6)

Change to stone

Rnds 6–14 dc (9 rnds)

Rnd 15 (dc2 into next st) 6 times (12)

Rnds 16–17 dc (2 rnds)

Rnd 18 (dc2tog) 6 times (6)

Rnds 19–28 dc (10 rnds)

Rnd 29 (dc2 into next st) 6 times (12)

Rnd 30 (dc1, dc2 into next st) 6 times (18)

Split into three 6 st rnds and work each as follows:

DIGITS

Rnds 1–4 dc (4 rnds)

Rnd 5 dc2tog, dc4 (5)

Rnds 6–7 dc (2 rnds)

Rnd 8 dc2tog, dc3 (4)

Rnd 9 dc2tog twice (2)

BACK DIGIT (optional)

Sl st traverse a 6 st root on to the back of the foot (see *Adding Details* in *Technicals*) and work as follows:

Rnds 1–2 dc (2 rnds)

Rnd 3 (dc2tog) 3 times (3)

WINGS

Work as *standard FLYING* with a colour change pattern of 3 sts cream, 2 sts black throughout.

BEAK

Working in stone

Ch15 and sl st to join into a circle

Rnd 1 dc

Rnd 2 (dc3, dc2tog) 3 times (12)

Rnd 3 dc

Rnd 4 (dc2, dc2tog) 3 times (9)

Rnds 5–6 dc (2 rnds)

Rnd 7 (dc1, dc2tog) 3 times (6)

Rnds 8–10 dc (3 rnds)

HEADDRESS

Into the top of head work three 6 st slip st spines in stone (see *Chain slip sts for feathers* in *Adding Details in Technicals section*). Finish by oversewing blue yarn into ends of spines.

TAIL (make 3)

Working in green

Ch18 and sl st to join into a circle

Rnd 1 dc

Rnd 2 (dc2, dc2 into next st) 6 times (24)

Rnds 3–5 dc (3 rnds)

Split into three 8 st rnds and work each as follows:

Rnds 1–8 dc (8 rnds)

Rnd 9 dc7, dc2 into next st (9)

Rnds 10–11 dc (2 rnds)

Rnd 12 dc8, dc2 into next st (10)

Rnd 13 dc

Rnd 14 (dc4, dc2 into next st) twice (12)

Rnds 15–16 dc (2 rnds)

Rnd 17 (dc3, dc2 into next st) 3 times (15)

Rnds 18–19 dc (2 rnds)

Rnd 20 (dc1, dc2tog) 5 times (10)

Rnd 21 (dc2tog) 5 times (5)

OCELLI (EYESPOTS) (make 9)

Working in blue

Begin by dc6 into foundation ring (see *Technicals*)

Change to camel

Rnd 1 (dc2 into next st) 6 times (12)

MAKING UP

See *Stuffing and Sewing* in the *Technicals* section, and the notes below.

NOTES

Sew the ocelli onto end of each tail prong. Sew two parts of the tail in the normal position side by side and the third one above them and centralised.

CAESAR
the Emperor Penguin

Caesar is a hairdresser. He snips and preens to sleek perfection, and in fact the only drawback to this talented penguin's salon is that his streamlined style is so honed that it often gets in the way of what the customer actually wants. Unless you know you can 'go short', and carry off blocky contrasts and 'pops' of colour, then you might want to steer clear of Caesar's, because even if you don't ask for his signature cut, you more often than not get it anyway.

YOU WILL NEED

Main colour: Black

Colour two: Cream

Colour three: Charcoal

Colour four: Yellow

See also *You will need* list in *Yarn and Other Materials* section, and *Abbreviations*.

BODY/NECK/HEAD

Starting in cream work as *standard* until

Rnd 6 (dc5, dc2 into next st) 6 times (42)

Rnd 7-8 dc21 black, dc21 cream

Rnd 9 dc1 cream, dc20 black, dc21 cream

Rnd 10 dc1 cream, dc4, dc2tog, (dc5, dc2tog) twice black, (dc5, dc2tog) 3 times cream (36)

Rnds 11-13 dc2 cream, dc16 black, dc18 cream (3 rnds)

Rnd 14 dc3 cream, dc15 black, dc18 cream

Rnd 15 dc3 cream, dc1, dc2tog, (dc4, dc2tog) twice black, (dc4, dc2tog) 3 times cream (30)

Rnd 16 dc3 cream, dc12 black, dc15 cream

Rnds 17-18 dc4 cream, dc11 black, dc15 cream (2 rnds)

Rnd 19 dc5 cream, dc10 black, dc15 cream

Rnd 20 dc3, dc2tog yellow, (dc3, dc2tog) twice black, (dc3, dc2tog) 3 times yellow (24)

Rnd 21 dc5 yellow, dc7 black, dc12 yellow

Next dc6 in yellow. Move st marker to this point and RESET.

Rnd 22 dc6 black, (dc2tog) 9 times yellow (15)

Rnd 23 dc2tog, dc4 black, (dc2tog) 4 times, dc1 yellow (10)

Rnd 24 dc5 black, dc5 yellow

Next dc5 in black. Move st marker to this point and RESET.

HEAD

Rnd 25 (dc2 into next st) 6 times yellow, (dc2 into next st) 3 times black, dc2 into next st yellow (20)

Rnd 26 (dc3, dc2 into next st) twice, dc3, dc2 into next st yellow, dc3, dc2 into next st, dc2 black, dc1, dc2 into next st, yellow (25)

Continue as standard in black.

LEGS

Work as *standard WADDLING* starting in cream and changing to charcoal after thighs and work FLIPPERS in black.

WINGS

Work as *standard SWIMMING*.

BEAK

Working in charcoal

Ch18 and sl st to join into a circle

Rnd 1 dc

Rnd 2 (dc4, dc2tog) 3 times (15)

Rnd 3 dc

Rnd 4 (dc2tog) 3 times, dc9 (12)

Rnds 5-6 dc

Rnd 7 (dc2, dc2tog) 3 times (9)

Rnds 8-9 dc

Rnd 10 (dc1, dc2tog) 3 times (6)

Rnds 11-12 dc

Rnd 13 (dc2tog) 3 times (3)

TAIL

Working in black

Ch24 and sl st to join into a circle

Rnds 1-4 dc (4 rnds)

Rnd 5 (dc2tog) 12 times (12)

Rnd 6 dc

Rnd 7 (dc2tog) 6 times (6)

MAKING UP

See *Stuffing and Sewing* in the *Technicals* section, note the *Order of Sewing* for penguin legs, and see the notes below.

NOTES

Stuff the beak and thighs.

ENID
the Long-eared Owl

At school, Enid's teachers always speculated that she was wise beyond her years and her breathy hoots might one day make history. So hard has she fought for what she believes in that she has had to sacrifice a lot of things on her flight path into Parliament. Her entire career she has kept her wide eyes firmly fixed on the glass ceiling above her, which she fully intends to fly straight through when she gets there. The moment she stood up in the debating society and proposed the motion 'the more mice I meet, the more I eat nuts', her family should have foreseen that she was a pretty extraordinary owl.

YOU WILL NEED

Main colour: Stone

Colour two: Chestnut

Colour three: Oatmeal

See also *You will need* list in *Yarn and Other Materials* section, and *Abbreviations*.

BODY/NECK/HEAD

Work as *standard* using a 4st stone, 2st chestnut colour pattern every other rnd throughout.

LEGS

Work as *standard GRASPING* starting in stone and changing to oatmeal at rnd 15. Work claws in chestnut.

WINGS

Work as *standard SOARING* in 4 st stone, 2st chestnut colour pattern throughout.

BEAK (worked flat)

Working in chestnut

Ch4, turn, dc3 back along ch, turn, dc2 back the other way.

EYES

Working in oatmeal

Begin by dc6 into foundation ring (see *Technicals*)

Rnd 1 (dc2 into next st) 6 times (12)

Rnd 2 (dc1, dc2 into next st) 6 times (18)

Rnd 3 dc9 in chestnut (this is an incomplete rnd)

EARS

Wrap chestnut yarn twice around your hand. Put hook through the head around a st where you would like to place the ears. Remove yarn from hand and yarn over with the four strands of yarn. Pull through, tie off and cut loops (like a tassel).

TAIL

Working in 4st stone, 2st chestnut colour pattern throughout.

Ch16 and sl st to join into a circle

Rnds 1–2 dc (2 rnds)

Rnd 3 (dc1, dc2 into next st) 8 times (24)

Rnds 4–5 dc (2 rnds)

Next split into three 8 st rnds and work right and left 8 st rnds as follows:

Rnds 6–9 dc (4 rnds)

Rnd 10 dc7, dc2 into next st (9)

Rnd 11 dc

Rnd 12 dc8, dc2 into next st (10)

Rnds 13–15 dc (3 rnds)

Rnd 16 (dc3, dc2tog) twice (8)

Rnd 17 (dc2, dc2tog) twice (6)

Rnd 18 (dc2tog) 3 times (3)

Work central 8 st rnd as follows:

Rnds 6–9 dc (4 rnds)

Rnd 10 dc7, dc2 into next st (9)

Rnds 11–14 dc (4 rnds)

Rnd 15 dc8, dc2 into next st (10)

Rnds 16–18 dc (3 rnds)

Rnd 19 (dc3, dc2tog) 2 times (8)

Rnd 20 (dc2, dc2tog) 2 times (6)

Rnd 21 (dc2tog) 3 times (3)

MAKING UP

See *Stuffing and Sewing* in the *Technicals* section, and the notes below.

NOTES

Sew th eyes onto the face with chestnut half rounds at the top and meeting in the middle. Sew the beak in between.

JACK
the Macaw

Jack has recently become a swashbuckling entertainer, following a dramatic fall from grace (off the stage and into the orchestra pit) on the opening night of his big break. A plausible Iago he ain't. It turns out he is far more lovable rogue than maligned plunderer, and the sound of fledglings' giddy peeping fills his big heart with tenderness, and that overwhelming emotion now safely locked up in his chest has superseded any desire to break a leg. Once his peg is strapped on and he's hobbling in front of the bouncy castle he'll walk the plank any number of times for giggling tweets.

YOU WILL NEED

Main colour: Yellow

Colour two: Blue

Colour three: Steel

Colour four: Black

Colour five: Cream

Colour six: Green

See also *You will need* list in *Yarn and Other Materials* section, and *Abbreviations*.

BODY/NECK/HEAD

Work as *standard* in yellow until

Rnd 24 dc5 yellow, dc5 blue

HEAD

Rnd 25 (dc2 into next st) 5 times yellow, (dc2 into next st) 5 times blue (20)

Rnd 26 (dc3, dc2 into next st) twice, dc2 yellow, dc1, dc2 into next st, (dc3, dc2 into next st) twice blue (25)

Rnd 27 (dc4, dc2 into next st) twice, dc2 yellow, dc2 ,dc2 into next st, (dc4, dc2 into next st) twice blue (30)

Rnd 28 (dc2, dc2 into next st) 4 times, dc2 yellow, dc2 into next st, (dc2, dc2 into next st) 5 times blue (40)

Rnd 29 dc18 black, dc22 blue

Rnds 30-31 dc18 cream, dc22 blue (2 rnds)

Rnd 32 dc8, dc2tog, dc8 cream, dc2tog, (dc8, dc2tog) twice blue (36)

Rnd 33 dc17 cream, dc19 green

Rnd 34 (dc4, dc2tog) twice, dc4 cream, dc2tog across both colours, (dc4, dc2tog) 3 times green (30)

Change to green

Rnd 35 (dc3, dc2tog) 6 times (24)

Rnd 36 (dc2, dc2tog) 6 times (18)

Rnd 37 dc

Rnd 38 (dc2tog) 9 times (9)

Rnd 39 (dc1, dc2tog) 3 times (6)

LEGS

Work as *standard CLIMBING* starting yellow and changing to steel after rnd 9.

WINGS

Work as *standard SOARING* in blue.

BEAK

Working in black

Ch24 and slst to join into a circle

Rnds 1-3 dc (3 rnds)

Rnd 4 (dc1, dc2tog) 8 times (16)

Rnd 5 (dc1, dc2tog) 5 times, dc1 (11)

Rnd 6 dc

Rnd 7 dc2tog, dc4, dc2 into next st, dc2, dc2tog (10)

Fold in half and oversew down the beak and add four over sts into the last space to create hook finish.

TAIL (worked in 2 parts)

Working in yellow

Ch16 and sl st to join into a circle

Rnds 1-2 dc (2 rnds)

Rnd 3 (dc1, dc2 into next st) 8 times (24)

Rnds 4-5 dc (2 rnds)

Split to three 8 st branches

Rnds 1-3 dc (3 rnds)

Rnd 4 dc7, dc2 into next st (9)

Rnds 5-7 dc (3 rnds)

Rnd 8 dc8, dc2 into next st (10)

Rnd 9-11 dc (3 rnds)

Rnd 12 (dc3, dc2tog) twice (8)

Rnd 13 (dc2, dc2tog) twice (6)

Rnd 14 (dc2tog) 3 times (3)

Working in blue

Ch16 and sl st to join into a circle

Rnds 1-6 dc (6 rnds)

Split into two 8 st rnds and work each as follows:

Rnds 1-4 dc (4 rnds)

Rnd 5 dc7, dc2 into next st (9)

Rnds 6-8 dc (3 rnds)

Rnd 9 dc8, dc2 into next st (10)

Rnds 10-12 dc (3 rnds)

Rnd 13 (dc3, dc2tog) twice (8)

Rnd 14 (dc2, dc2tog) twice (6)

Rnd 15 (dc2tog) 3 times (3)

MAKING UP

See *Stuffing and Sewing* in the *Technicals* section, and the notes below.

NOTES

Sew the blue tail on top of the yellow tail. Stuff the beak and sew open onto the face. Lightly stuff the thighs.

PETRA
the Rockhopper Penguin

Petra is a meticulous and conscientious penguin with one big contradiction – she struggles to fly the nest more mornings than not. With her leather jacket on and naturally blonde mop-top, she's a penguin with the looks and talent to make waves. That she isn't a lark annoys no one more than herself, and it's easy to imagine her self-chastisement about not being an early bird as she applies her make-up in the rear-view mirror on the long commute to work each day.

YOU WILL NEED

Main colour: Cream

Colour two: Black

Colour three: Oatmeal

Colour four: Orange

Colour five: Yellow

See also *You will need* list in *Yarn and Other Materials* section, and *Abbreviations*.

BODY/NECK/HEAD

Starting in cream work as *standard* until

Rnd 6 (dc5, dc2 into next st) 6 times (42)

Rnds 7-8 dc21 black, dc21 cream (2 rnds)

Rnd 9 dc1 cream, dc20 black, dc21 cream

Rnd 10 dc1 cream, dc4, dc2tog, (dc5, dc2tog) twice black, (dc5, dc2tog) 3 times cream (36)

Rnds 11-13 dc2 cream, dc16 black, dc18 cream (3 rnds)

Rnd 14 dc3 cream, dc15 black, dc18 cream

Rnd 15 dc3 cream, dc1, dc2tog, (dc4, dc2tog) twice black, (dc4, dc2tog) 3 times cream (30)

Rnd 16 dc3 cream, dc12 black, dc15 cream

Rnds 17-18 dc4 cream, dc11 black, dc15 cream (2 rnds)

Rnd 19 dc5 cream, dc10 black, dc15 cream

Rnd 20 dc3, dc2tog cream, (dc3, dc2tog) twice black, (dc3, dc2tog) 3 times cream (24)

Rnd 21 dc5 cream, dc7 black, dc12 cream

Next dc6 in cream. Move st marker to this point and RESET

Rnd 22 dc6 black, (dc2tog) 9 times cream (15)

Rnd 23 dc5 black, (dc2tog) 5 times cream (10)

Continue as standard in black.

LEGS

Work as *standard WADDLING* starting in cream and changing to oatmeal after thighs.

WINGS

Work as *standard SWIMMING*.

BEAK

Working in orange

Ch18 and sl st to join into a circle

Rnd 1 dc

Rnd 2 (dc4, dc2tog) 3 times (15)

Rnd 3 dc

Rnd 4 (dc2tog) 3 times, dc9 (12)

Rnds 5-6 dc (2 rnds)

Rnd 7 (dc2, dc2tog) 3 times (9)

Rnds 8-9 dc (2 rnds)

Rnd 10 (dc1, dc2tog) 3 times (6)

Rnds 11-12 dc (2 rnds)

Rnd 13 (dc2tog) 3 times (3)

TAIL

Working in black

Ch24 and sl st to join into a circle

Rnds 1-4 dc (4 rnds)

Rnd 5 (dc2tog) 12 times (12)

Rnd 6 dc

Rnd 7 (dc2tog) 6 times (6)

HEADDRESS

Working in yellow

Slip st two 12 st, two 15 st and one 18 st slip st spines into two tufts on the top of head. See *Slip st chains for feathers* in *Technicals*.

MAKING UP

See *Stuffing and Sewing* in the *Technicals* section, note the *Order of Sewing* for penguin legs and see the notes below.

NOTES

Stuff the beak and thighs.

BEN
the Kingfisher

Ben has a sideways smile that has always sent the girls a-flutter, and is exactly the kind of flirt that has them pecking at each other in his trail. You'll have to try quite hard to find out anything about him that he doesn't want you to know, and so tightly held are certain cards that it leads some to wonder about whether he only whispers all his thoughts to the fish. His staunchly competitive character hides just below the surface of his immaculately presented plumage; so whatever you do don't challenge him to a fishing competition because you might just get more than you bargained for.

YOU WILL NEED

Main colour: Blue

Colour two: Camel

Colour three: Orange

Colour four: Steel

Colour five: Cream

See also *You will need* list in *Yarn and Other Materials* section, and *Abbreviations*.

BODY/NECK/HEAD

Work as *standard* in camel until rnd 23

Rnd 24 dc5 cream, dc5 blue

HEAD

Rnd 25 (dc2 into next st) 5 times cream, (dc2 into next st) 5 times blue (20)

Rnd 26 (dc3, dc2 into next st) twice, dc2 cream, dc1, dc2 into next st, (dc3, dc2 into next) twice blue (25)

Rnd 27 (dc4, dc2 into next st) 5 times blue (30)

Rnd 28 (dc2, dc2 into next st) 4 times, dc2 cream, dc2 into next st, (dc2, dc2 into next) 5 times blue (40)

Rnds 29-31 dc18 camel, dc 22 blue (3 rnds)

Rnd 32 dc8, dc2tog, dc8 camel, dc2tog, (dc8, dc2tog) twice blue (36)

Rnd 33 dc 17 camel, dc 19 blue

Continue as *standard* in blue

LEGS

Working in orange

Ch12 and sl st to join into a circle.

Rnds 1-3 dc (3 rnds)

Rnd 4 (dc2, dc2tog) 3 times (9)

Rnd 5 (dc1, dc2tog) 3 times (6)

Rnds 6-7 dc (2 rnds)

Rnd 8 (dc2 into next st) 6 times (12)

Rnds 9-10 dc (2 rnds)

Rnd 11 (dc2tog) 6 times (6)

Rnds 12-15 dc (4 rnds)

Rnd 16 (dc2 into next st) 6 times (12)

Rnd 17 (dc1, dc2 into next st) 6 times (18)

Split into three 6st branches and rejoin and work each as follows:

DIGITS

Rnds 1-3 dc

Rnd 4 dc2tog, dc4 (5)

Rnds 5-6 dc

Rnd 7 dc2tog, dc3 (4)

WINGS

Work as *standard FLYING* in blue.

BEAK

Working in steel

Ch18 and sl st to join into a circle

Rnds 1-4 dc (4 rnds)

Rnd 5 (dc4, dc2tog) 3 times (15)

Rnds 6-8 dc (3 rnds)

Rnd 9 (dc3, dc2tog) 3 times (12)

Rnds 10-11 dc (2 rnds)

Rnd 12 (dc2, dc2tog) 3 times (9)

Rnds 13-14 dc (2 rnds)

Rnd 15 (dc1, dc2tog) 3 times (6)

Rnd 16 dc

Rnd 17 (dc2tog) 3 times (3)

TAIL

Working in camel

Ch18 and sl st to join into a circle

Change to blue

Rnds 1-2 dc (2 rnds)

Rnd 3 (dc2, dc2 into next st) 6 times (24)

Rnd 4 dc

Split into three 8 st rnds and work each as follows:

Rnds 1-4 dc (4 rnds)

Rnd 5 (dc2tog) 4 times (4)

MAKING UP

See *Stuffing and Sewing* in the *Technicals* section, and the notes below.

NOTES

Stuff the beak and sew on slightly flattened. Lightly stuff the thighs.

ANIK
the Snowy Owl

A prolific author, Anik is a solitary owl who has spent her life swooping in and out of lots of social groups never really finding one to call home. Secretive, smart and sophisticated, she remains a beautiful enigma to all her readers who have little idea of who lies behind her pseudonym. Rumour has it that she spends her time caged up and bent over a laptop clawing out her next 5000 gripping words. Life as this best-selling, self-published writer is a nocturnal one and, even if you are mid-conversation, as soon as the sun comes up she disappears in a single flap of her black and white wings leaving you with a flash of fifty shades of grey.

YOU WILL NEED

Main colour: Cream

Colour two: Charcoal

Colour three: Silver

See also *You will need* list in *Yarn and Other Materials* section, and *Abbreviations*.

BODY/NECK/HEAD

Work as *standard* using a 4 st cream, 2st charcoal colour pattern every other rnd throughout.

LEGS

Work as *standard GRASPING* starting in cream and working loop st every 4th st and changing to silver at rnd 15. Work *CLAWS* in charcoal.

WINGS

Work as *standard SOARING* in 4st cream, 2st charcoal colour pattern throughout.

BEAK (WORKED FLAT)

Working in silver

Ch4, turn, dc3 back along ch, turn, dc2 back the other way.

EYES

Working in cream

Begin by dc6 into foundation ring (see *Technicals*)

Rnd 1 (dc2 into next st) 6 times (12)

Rnd 2 (dc1, dc2 into next st) 6 times (18)

Rnd 3 dc9 in charcoal (this is an incomplete rnd)

TAIL

Working in 4st cream, 2st charcoal colour pattern throughout.

Ch16 and sl st to join into a circle

Rnds 1–2 dc (2 rnds)

Rnd 3 (dc1, dc2 into next st) 8 times (24)

Rnds 4–5 dc (2 rnds)

Next split into three 8 st rnds and work right and left 8 st rnds as follows:

Rnds 6–9 dc (4 rnds)

Rnd 10 dc7, dc2 into next st (9)

Rnd 11 dc

Rnd 12 dc8, dc2 into next st (10)

Rnds 13–15 dc (3 rnds)

Rnd 16 (dc3, dc2tog) twice (8)

Rnd 17 (dc2, dc2tog) twice (6)

Rnd 18 (dc2tog) 3 times (3)

Work central 8 st rnd as follows:

Rnds 6–9 dc (4 rnds)

Rnd 10 dc7, dc2 into next st (9)

Rnds 11–14 dc (4 rnds)

Rnd 15 dc8, dc2 into next st (10)

Rnds 16–18 dc (3 rnds)

Rnd 19 (dc3, dc2tog) 2 times (8)

Rnd 20 (dc2, dc2tog) 2 times (6)

Rnd 21 (dc2tog) 3 times (3)

MAKING UP

See *Stuffing and Sewing* in the *Technicals* section, and the notes below.

NOTES

Sew th eyes onto the face with charcoal – half rounds at top and meeting in the middle. Sew the beak in between.

GILBERT
the Pheasant

Gilbert is a classic country gentleman running through life being as politically incorrect as he can get away with. With his home-brewed sloe-gin filled hipflask tucked under his wing, he pecks at people's good humour with his controversial wit until he has the room in a complete flap, declares he's won the argument, and moves on. His confrontational spatting is far more than just a game; it's a way of life! Be wary of starting up a conversation with this confident cock, as whether man, beast or bird he's sure to find just the issues to get to you, leaving you offended, angry and gunning for him.

YOU WILL NEED

Main colour: Chestnut

Colour two: Camel

Colour three: Stone

Colour four: Oatmeal

Colour five: Green

Colour six: Orange

Colour seven: Cream

See also *You will need* list in *Yarn and Other Materials* section, and *Abbreviations*.

BODY/NECK/HEAD

Work as *standard* in a 3st camel, 2st chestnut pattern until

Rnds 16, 18 and 20 work 2st camel, 2st chestnut pattern

Rnds 17, 19 and 21 work in 3st camel, 2st chestnut pattern

Change to cream

Rnd 22 (dc2tog) 9 times, dc6 (15)

Rnd 23 (dc2tog) 5 times, dc5 (10)

Change to green

Rnd 24 dc

Rnd 25 (dc2 into next st) 5 times orange, (dc2 into next st) 5 times green (20)

Rnd 26 (dc3, dc2 into next st) twice, dc2 orange, dc1, dc2 into next st, (dc3, dc2 into next st) twice green (25)

Rnd 27 (dc4, dc2 into next st) twice, dc2 orange, dc2, dc2 into next st, (dc4, dc2 into next st) twice green (30)

Rnd 28 (dc2, dc2 into next st) 4 times, dc2 orange, dc2 into next st, (dc2, dc2 into next st) 5 times green (40)

Rnds 29–31 dc18 orange, dc22 green (3 rnds)

Rnd 32 dc8, dc2tog, dc8 orange, dc2tog, (dc8, dc2tog) twice green (36)

Rnd 33 dc17 orange, dc19 green

Rnd 34 (dc4, dc2tog) twice, dc4 orange, dc2tog across both colours, (dc4, dc2tog) 3 times green (30)

Change to green

Rnd 35 (dc3, dc2tog) 6 times (24)

Rnd 36 (dc2, dc2tog) 6 times (18)

Rnd 37 dc

Rnd 38 (dc2tog) 9 times (9)

Rnd 39 (dc1, dc2tog) 3 times (6)

LEGS

Work as *standard PERCHING* but with 6 rnds *TIBIA* and 7 rnds *TARSUS* starting in chestnut and changing to stone after thigh.

WINGS

Work as *standard FLAPPING* in chestnut.

BEAK

Working in oatmeal

Ch8 and sl st to join into a circle

Rnds 1–2 dc (2 rnds)

Rnd 3 dc6, dc2tog (7)

Rnd 4 dc5, dc2tog (6)

Rnd 5 dc4, dc2tog (5)

Rnd 6 dc

Rnd 7 dc3, dc2tog (4)

Rnd 8 dc2, dc2tog (3)

TAIL

Work in a 4 rnds oatmeal, 1 rnd chestnut colour pattern throughout.

Ch16 and sl st to join into a circle

Rnds 1–6 dc (6 rnds)

Split into two 8 st rnds and work each as follows:

Rnd 1–3 dc (3rnds)

Rnd 4 dc7, dc2 into next st (9)

Rnd 5–7 dc (3 rnds)

Rnd 8 dc8, dc2 into next (10)

Rnd 9–11 dc (3 rnds)

Rnd 12 (dc3, dc2tog) twice (8)

Rnd 13 (dc2, dc2tog) twice (6)

Rnd 14 (dc2tog) 3 times (3)

Rnd 15 dc2tog, dc1 (2)

MAKING UP

See *Stuffing and Sewing* in the *Technicals* section, and the notes below.

NOTES

Stuff the beak and thighs. Sew the tail up the back a few sts to position in an alert pose.

OSCAR
the Penguin

Oscar is a highly respected marine biologist. His unpretentious thoughts on sardine sandwiches, which became a published paper, now have him lecturing across the globe and making celebrity appearances on reality TV shows. He doesn't really know how he ended up where he is in life. It all started with a near-death incident with a coughing squid, and now it looks like his blog has gone viral and even his Friday night fish-tank cleaning ritual is no longer sacred.

YOU WILL NEED

Main colour: Cream

Colour two: Black

Colour three: Orange

Colour four: Yellow

See also *You will need* list in *Yarn and Other Materials* section, and *Abbreviations*.

BODY/NECK/HEAD

Starting in cream work as *standard* until

Rnd 6 (dc5, dc2 into next st) 6 times (42)

Rnds 7–8 dc21 black, dc21 cream (2 rnds)

Rnd 9 dc1 cream, dc20 black, dc21 cream

Rnd 10 dc1 cream, dc4, dc2tog, (dc5, dc2tog) twice black, (dc5, dc2tog) 3 times cream

Rnds 11–13 dc2 cream, dc16 black, dc18 cream (3 rnds)

Rnd 14 dc3 cream, dc15 black, dc18 cream

Rnd 15 dc3 cream, dc1, dc2tog, (dc4, dc2tog) twice black, (dc4, dc2tog) 3 times cream (30)

Rnd 16 dc3 cream, dc12 black, dc15 cream

Rnds 17–18 dc4 cream, dc11 black, dc15 cream (2 rnds)

Rnd 19 dc5 cream, dc10 black, dc15 cream

Rnd 20 dc3, dc2tog cream, (dc3, dc2tog) twice black, (dc3, dc2tog) 3 times cream (24)

Rnd 21 dc5 cream, dc7 black, dc12 cream

Next dc6 in cream. Move st marker to this point and RESET

Rnd 22 dc6 black, (dc2tog) 9 times cream (15)

Rnd 23 dc2tog, dc4 black, (dc2tog) 4 times, dc1 cream (10)

Rnd 24 dc5 black, dc5 cream

Next dc5 in black. Move st marker to this point and RESET

HEAD

Rnd 25 (dc2 into next st) 5 times cream, (dc2 into next st) 5 times black (20)

Rnd 26 (dc3, dc2 into next st) twice, dc2 cream, dc1, dc2 into next st, (dc3, dc2 into next st) twice black (25)

Rnd 27 (dc4, dc2 into next st) twice, dc2 cream, dc2, dc2 into next st, (dc4, dc2 into next st) twice black (30)

Rnd 28 (dc2, dc2 into next st) 4 times, dc2 cream, dc2 into next st, (dc2, dc2 into next st) 5 times black (40)

Rnds 29–31 dc18 cream, dc22 black (3 rnds)

Rnd 32 dc8, dc2tog, dc8 cream, dc2tog, (dc8, dc2tog) twice black (36)

Rnd 33 dc17 cream, dc19 black

Rnd 34 (dc4, dc2tog) twice, dc4 cream dc2tog across both colours, (dc4, dc2tog) 3 times black (30)

Continue as *standard* in black.

LEGS

Work as *standard WADDLING* starting in cream and changing to orange after thigh.

WINGS

Work as *standard SWIMMING*.

BEAK

Working in yellow

Ch6 and sl st to join into a circle

Rnd 1 dc

Rnd 2 (dc1, dc2tog) twice (4)

Rnd 3 dc

Rnd 4 (dc2tog) twice (2)

TAIL

Working in black

Ch24 and sl st to join into a circle

Rnds 1–4 dc (4 rnds)

Rnd 5 (dc2tog) 12 times (12)

Rnd 6 dc

Rnd 7 (dc2tog) 6 times (6)

MAKING UP

See *Stuffing and Sewing* in the *Technicals* section.

NOTES

Stuff the thighs.

JORGE
the Jay

Gorgeous Jorge is a singer-songwriter who once produced a catchy one-line tune and now the whole world thinks he's something special. He was in the right place at the right time ten years ago and was delivered the chance for a home-run that would provide him with a nest egg for life. But, life is tough when everyone in the business compares what you do now with something critically acclaimed that you did partially by accident a long time ago. To stay relevant against constantly shifting opinion your feathers have to grow bolder, your beak a bit harder, and you have to start to believe that maybe you are somewhat extraordinary after all.

YOU WILL NEED

Main colour: Blue

Colour two: Cream

Colour three: Steel

Colour four: Charcoal

See also *You will need* list in *Yarn and Other Materials* section, and *Abbreviations*.

BODY/NECK/HEAD

Work as *standard* in cream until

HEAD

Rnd 25 (dc2 into next st) 4 times, dc1 charcoal, (dc2 into next st) 5 times blue (19)

Rnd 26 dc1 charcoal, (dc2, dc2 into the next st) twice, dc2 cream, dc1 charcoal, dc2 into next st (dc3, dc2 into next st) twice blue (24)

Rnd 27 dc1, charcoal, dc3, dc2 into next st, dc4, dc2 into next st, dc1 cream, dc1 charcoal, (dc2, dc2 into next st) 4 times blue (30)

Rnd 28 dc1 charcoal, dc1, dc2 into next st (dc2, dc2 into next st) 3 times, dc1 cream, dc1 charcoal, dc2 into next st (dc2, dc2 into next st) 5 times blue (40)

Rnds 29–31 dc1 charcoal, dc16 cream, dc1 charcoal, dc22 blue (3 rnds)

Rnd 32 dc1 charcoal, dc6, dc2tog, dc8 cream, dc1 charcoal, dc2tog, (dc8, dc2tog) twice blue (36)

Rnd 33 dc17 charcoal, dc19 blue

Continue as standard in blue

LEGS

Work as *standard PERCHING* starting in cream and changing to steel after thigh.

WINGS

Work as *standard FLYING* in blue.

BEAK

Working in steel

Ch12 and sl st to join into a circle

Rnd 1 dc10, dc2tog (11)

Rnd 2 dc9, dc2tog (10)

Rnd 3 dc8, dc2tog (9)

Rnd 4 dc7, dc2tog (8)

Rnd 5 dc6, dc2tog (7)

Rnd 6 dc5, dc2tog (6)

Rnd 7 dc4, dc2tog (5)

Rnd 8 dc3, dc2tog (4)

Rnd 9 dc2, dc2tog (3)

Rnd 10 dc

TAIL

Work in a 4 rnds blue, 1 rnd charcoal colour pattern throughout

Ch16 and sl st to join into a circle

Rnds 1–6 dc (6 rnds)

Split into two 8 st rnds and work each as follows:

Rnds 1–3 dc (3 rnds)

Rnd 4 dc7, dc2 into next st (9)

Rnds 5–7 dc (3 rnds)

Rnd 8 dc8, dc2 into next st (10)

Rnds 9–11 dc (3 rnds)

Rnd 12 (dc3, dc2tog) twice (8)

Rnd 13 (dc2, dc2tog) twice (6)

Rnd 14 (dc2tog) 3 times (3)

Rnd 15 dc2tog, dc1 (2)

CREST

Working in blue

Ch30 and sl st to join into a circle

Rnds 1–2 dc (2 rnds)

Rnd 3 (dc2tog) 6 times, dc18 (24)

Rnd 4 (dc10, dc2tog) twice (22)

Rnd 5 (dc9, dc2tog) twice (20)

Rnd 6 (dc8, dc2tog) twice (18)

Rnd 7 (dc4, dc2tog) 3 times (15)

Rnd 8 (dc2tog) 3 times, dc9 (12)

Rnd 9 (dc2tog) twice, dc8 (10)

Rnd 10 dc

Rnd 11 (dc2tog) 5 times (5)

Rnd 12 (dc2tog) twice, dc1 (3)

MAKING UP

See *Stuffing and Sewing* in the *Technicals* section, and the notes below.

NOTES

Lightly stuff the crest, beak and thighs.

TECHNICALS

In the following pages I aim to equip a beginner with the tools to make any or all of the entire menagerie of animals and birds. Even if you are a seasoned crocheter, take the time to glance over the instructions, as certain methods for techniques, such as decreasing and colour changing, may be new to you.

BASIC SKILLS

COUNTING

A basic skill to keep yourself on track and get yourself out of trouble is counting the number of stitches you have in a round. After each round involving increasing or decreasing instructions the number at the end of the line in brackets will indicate how many stitches you should have to work with next. If you complete a round and this number is incorrect, simply pull back the round to your marker on the previous round and rework it.

MARKING

Use a stitch marker to keep track of the end of each round as you work. I recommend hooking in a piece of contrast yarn approximately 15cm (6in) long after the end of rnd 2; as you get back around to it pull it through forwards or backwards over your stitches to weave a marker up your fabric. You will start to appreciate how spiralled the shape you are working is and understand that the beginning of the next round isn't where you might presume it was. The marker can be removed when you have finished with no damage to the fabric. See *Working the Stitches*.

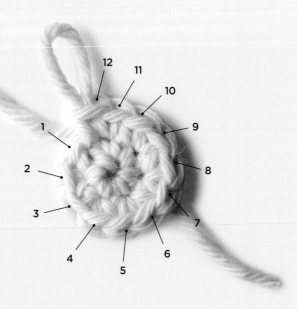

RIGHT SIDE AND WRONG SIDE OF FABRIC

An essential skill is learning to recognize the right side (RS) from the wrong side (WS) of the fabric. If you are right-handed and crocheting with the RS facing outwards, you will be moving in an anticlockwise direction (that is, from right to left) around the piece you are making, pushing the hook into the fabric from the outside to the inside. It is very easy to have accidentally learned to crochet holding your work WS outwards facing (I did it myself), but with these birds, and especially their legs, you won't have the option of turning them WS-in once completed because the rounds are too small, so now's the time to alter your technique! Left-handed people should work clockwise rather than anti-clockwise.

RIGHT SIDE   WRONG SIDE

INSIDE OUT

When making complex colour changes that require you to run the yarn behind the fabric on the inside of the part, make sure your don't pull the threads too tight when changing the colour as this will pucker the fabric and change the shape of the part.

ABBREVIATIONS

ch: chain. A chain is the most fundamental of all crochet stitches.

dc: double crochet. Using the double crochet stitch creates a compact and dense fabric. (NB: this is known as sc – single crochet – in US terminology.)

dc2tog: double crochet two stitches together (decrease by one stitch).

rnd: round. A round is a complete rotation in a spiral back to your stitch marker. With these patterns you DO NOT slip stitch at the end of a round to make a circle, but instead continue straight onto the next round in a spiral.

RS: right side. The right side of your fabric will show small 'V' shapes in horizontal lines and will form the outside of the animal.

sl st: slip stitch. This is the simplest crochet stitch.

st(s): stitch(es). You can count your stitches around the edge of your fabric.

WS: wrong side. The wrong side of your fabric will have vertical spiralling furrows. This is where you have all the ends or strands of yarn, and it forms the inside of the animal.

WORKING THE STITCHES

SLIP KNOT	CHAIN (ch)	SLIP STITCH (sl st) (to join into circle)

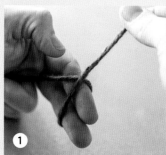  

SLIP KNOT

1. Make a loop in the yarn.
2. Pull the yarn through the loop.
3. Place your hook through the loop and tighten.

CHAIN (ch)

1. Make a slip knot.
2. Wrap yarn over the hook (yarn over) and pull through the loop close around the hook but not too tight.
3. Repeat until desired length.

SLIP STITCH (sl st)

1. Insert the hook into the stitch closest to the slip knot.
2. Yarn over hook.
3. Pull the yarn through the stitch and loop in one motion.

FOUNDATION RING (dc6 into ring)	DOUBLE CROCHET (dc)	DECREASE (dc2tog)

FOUNDATION RING (dc6 into ring)

1. Make a slip knot and chain two stitches.

2. Insert the hook into the first chain stitch and work a double crochet stitch six times into this same stitch, working over the tail end of yarn.

3. Pull tightly on the tail of the yarn to close the centre of the ring.

DOUBLE CROCHET (dc)

1. Insert the hook through the stitch (both loops).

2. Yarn over and pull through the stitch.

3. Yarn over again and pull through both loops to end with one stitch.

   NB: US crocheters will know this stitch as single crochet (sc).

DECREASE (dc2tog)

1. Insert the hook through the front loop only of the stitch (two loops on the hook).

2. Insert the hook through the front loop of the next stitch (three loops on the hook).

3. Yarn over hook and pull through first two loops on the hook, then yarn over and pull through both remaining loops to complete the double crochet decrease.

COLOUR CHANGING	RESET	LOOP/FUR STITCH

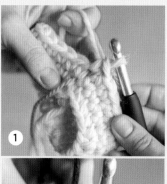

COLOUR CHANGING

1. Insert the hook through the next stitch, yarn over and pull through the stitch.

2. Yarn over with the new colour and complete the double crochet stitch with this new yarn.

3. Continue with this new colour, leaving the original colour to the back of the work. Cut if a one-off colour change or run on the WS of the fabric if colour changing back to it.

NB: You do this colour change at the end of the stitch before the one that you are working in a new colour. For example: Rnd 1 dc6 black, dc6 cream, dc 6 black.

After working 5 complete dc sts in black you would use the above steps to finish your 6th dc st moving from black to cream before working 5 full sts in cream, and again finishing the 6th st with the step above to move back to black.

RESET

1. Remove your existing stitch marker from your fabric.

2. Follow instructions as given in the pattern and then replace the marker once you have completed these sts.

3. Regards this new position as a fresh start and continue to work the pattern, pulling through the marker yarn with your final yarn over of every rnd to keep it moving up your work with you.

NB: I have used this reset technique in a couple of patterns in order to make following the instructions for the colour changing easier. Due to the nature of the spiral form the colours creep diagonally, and this reset allows me to simply split the colour changing into two blocks rather than fragment it over a rnd.

LOOP/FUR STITCH

1. Wrap the yarn from front to back over the thumb of your non-hook hand.

2. Insert the hook into the stitch and yarn over with the yarn behind your thumb.

3. Pull through leaving a loop on the WS and complete the double crochet stitch with a yarn over and pull through the two loops back to one.

4. Work frequency as directed in pattern.

SPLITTING A ROUND

BRANCHING ROUNDS

CHAIN SPLIT (CLIMBING LEG)

1. Count X sts back from the working loop as stated in the pattern.

2. Cross rnd and double crochet into this st on RS.

3. After completing instruction for this new smaller rnd, rejoin into the st that would have been worked next.

1. Following a split off of some sts rejoin into the st that would have been worked next.

2. Continue to work all the sts on that main rnd as instructed.

3. Once again split off this rnd into two smaller ones (this can get a bit fiddly so keep your tension loose).

1. Chain 6 sts from your current st.

2. Sl st to join in middle of the other side of the rnd.

3. You will then work one side of the chain, and afterwards rejoin and work into the other side to create a T-shape from the leg with the sts worked outwards from that central foundation chain.

PERCHING LEG

All leg patterns in the book will require you to split a larger rnd into multiple smaller rnds. You may find this diagram helpful when visualising this technique, but remember that the numbers represent the number of sts in that rnd.

Here an 18st rnd is split into 3 rnds of 6sts

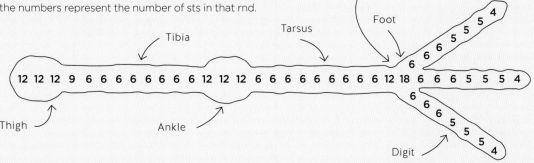

Tibia

Tarsus

Foot

Thigh

Ankle

Digit

ADDING DETAILS

Some of the feather and claw details are added once the main work of crocheting and assembling the toy is complete. As emphasized at the beginning of this book, this optional fourth claw is easy once you get the hang of it, so even if you are a beginner it's worth having a go at mastering this very useful technique. Once you have made the root on the fabric as per these steps you use this as a starting round to crochet out from.

SLIP STITCH TRAVERSE ROOT (OPTIONAL FOURTH CLAW)	CHAIN LOOPS FOR FEATHERS	CHAIN SLIP STITCHES FOR FEATHERS

1. Make a slip knot and insert the hook into the fabric around a stitch.

2. Yarn over and pull through the fabric and loop in one motion.

3. Move across the fabric in a circle making X sts in a ring to create root (here 6 sts).

   NB: This example has been worked in a contrasting colour to make the steps obvious, but it is always used in a matching colour in the patterns.

1. Make a slip knot and insert the hook through the fabric at the desired position of the first loop.

2. Dc through the fabric to secure and then * chain the number of stitches stated in the pattern. Attach the chain back to the fabric with a dc approximately every other stitch and row space away from the last one.

3. Repeat from *.

1. Make a slip knot and insert the hook through the fabric at the desired position of the first spine.

2. Dc through the fabric to secure and then chain the number of sts stated in the pattern.

3. Slip st back down that chain and repeat as instructed in the pattern.

STUFFING AND SEWING

When stuffing your birds less is definitely more. You want to show off the shape of the body and not make them firm and stiff, so proceed with caution and stuff tiny pinches of fluff into the thighs. Much of the appeal with this collection comes from the drape of the body, which is created through a combination of the luxury yarn and light-handed stuffing. Once you have crocheted the pieces and pushed the stuffing into them, you will need to roll and manipulate the parts in your hands to spread the stuffing evenly and ensure the best shape.

STUFFING THE BODIES

All the bodies are stuffed gently to fill out the shape and chest, but to retain their supple feel. I would advise stuffing the body before you proceed to making the head, especially with the birds using colour changes (but don't panic if you get carried away and forget as it is just about possible to stuff them afterwards with a bit of patience and a good pokey stick). With the long-necked birds I have not stuffed the necks so as to retain their floppy nature, but this does mean the heads loll forwards to rest their beaks on their chests.

STUFFING THE HEADS

All the heads are stuffed at the point at which you decrease to 9 stitches. Any stuffing required for beaks, crowns and combs is given in the individual patterns.

OVER STUFFED   JUST RIGHT

STUFFING THE LEGS AND FINISHING THE FEET

While it is not essential to stuff the thighs of any of the birds, on some it will be recommended in the pattern that you do so. I feel the waddling legs of the penguins in particular benefit from a small pinch of stuffing to fill them out before sewing or crocheting across the top and sewing into position. Sew at the recommended angle to ensure your birds are self-supporting when sitting up (see *Sewing on Legs and Tail*).

TAILS

Finish the tail by sewing your ch st start flat and closed and then oversew the tail onto the back horizontally. In general, I have not stuffed the tail with the exception of a few birds which will have instructions in the pattern.

SEWING IN ENDS

When sewing in your ends simply thread onto a darning needle and sew back inside the part and then secure. It will be much easier to get a neat finish if you remember to leave a longish thread whenever you join or finish with a colour or start and complete a part.

ORDER OF SEWING

1. Line up the chest shaping and then backstitch the beak in middle of the face (see *Sewing on beaks*).

2. Backstitch your wings into position in the desired location (see opposite).

3. Oversew your legs into position.

4. Oversew a flat tail horizontally across back.

   Add the extras.

NB: The penguins are an exception to this rule and their conjoined legs should be centered in the black stitches and then oversewn onto the last all cream round.

SEWING ON WINGS

Sew wings in place in any of the three positions shown. I would recommend backstitching around the marked stitches and oversewing several stitches into either end to strengthen and hinge them, in case little hands want to flap the wings to make their favourite bird fly.

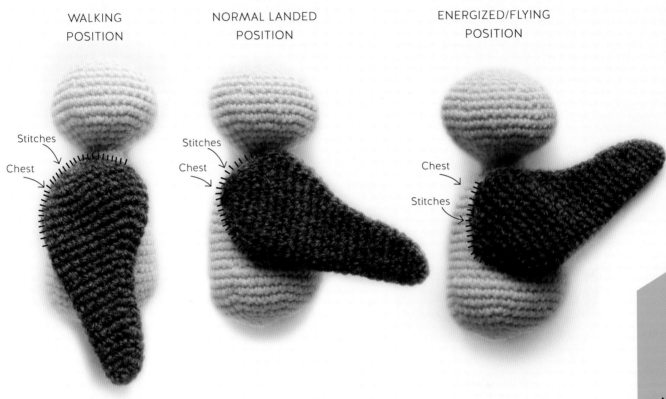

WALKING POSITION

NORMAL LANDED POSITION

ENERGIZED/FLYING POSITION

Stitches
Chest
Stitches
Chest
Chest
Stitches

SEWING ON LEGS AND TAIL

Oversew your tail and legs into position at these marked places to ensure the best proportions on your bird. I would recommend oversewing right around the piece to ensure that it is very securely attached.

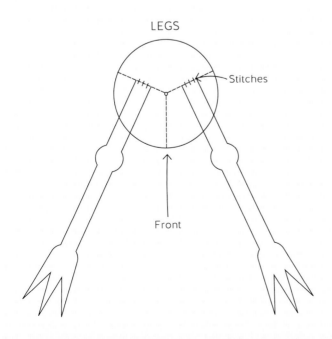

LEGS

Stitches

Front

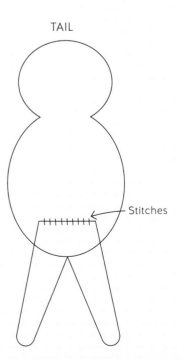

TAIL

Stitches

CREATING CHARACTER

When you start to sew on the face details of your bird his or her personality will really begin to emerge. Take your time to get this right; don't be afraid to cut it all off and start again (I do this frequently when working on a new animal).

SEWING ON EXTRAS
(wattles, snoods and combs)

Follow the instructions for the beak when sewing on stuffed parts that have open bottoms. Ensure that all small parts are very securely fastened on with plenty of oversewing.

SLEEPY-EYED   CROSS-EYED   BEADY-EYED   BIG-EYED

SEWING ON BEAKS

There are many different styles of beak, some stuffed and sewn on open, some sewn flat and then oversewn in (such as Robin) and some worked entirely flat and then sewn on (all three owls).

This is the standard method, unless instructions are otherwise stated in pattern:

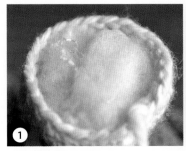

1. Lightly stuff the beak.

2. Sew into the fabric down through a ch st on the beak and into the head fabric and then up through both fabrics two sts along, and then sew back down one st behind this (backstitch).

3. Continue to backstitch around the edge into the ch so this edge lies flat on the head fabric.

SEWING ON EYES

When sewing the eyes I have used a simple method of two wraps of black yarn running vertically through the same stitches across two rows. Dora the Wood Pigeon's are an exception to this general rule, worked horizontally to create a sleepy character. Using more wraps to create bigger eyes will make the bird look cuter or younger. Using thinner yarn or just wrapping around on row of stitches will create beady eyes. Sewing the eyes close together will give a different style than if they are positioned on the side of the head.

My advice would be to play with the positioning to find out how you prefer the style of the eyes, but in general split the face into thirds to position and sew them on after your beak is in place.

1. Secure yarn at top of desired eye position.

2. Sew into fabric two rnds down and back up through the top of the secured yarn.

3. Repeat twice (or until you get the desired eye size).

WASHING

If made in natural yarn and stuffed with synthetic stuffing material, the animals can either be washed by hand or on a gentle cold machine cycle. Please be aware that if you opt to use beans, pellets or sand in your toys this may make them unwashable; you would need to sponge the surface clean.

SAFETY

Your animal will only be as safe as you make it, so don't skimp on the stitches when sewing up. With ears and legs, I oversew all the way around the edges – you really can't sew them too much! I have also only used yarn to sew on eyes. You could use beads or buttons as an alternative. Never use toy safety eyes, beads or buttons on an animal intended for a child under three years old; you should always embroider the details instead.

MAKE THOSE TAIL FEATHERS

1. Alan's is the most common two-prong tail in this book. This tail type is shared with Dora, Ernest, Henry, Vince, Dave, Mateo, Scott, Meghan, Robin and Jorge

2. Elvis has an average length flared three-prong tail shared by Ina, Sophia, Emily, Abraham and Gianni

3. Barney and all the owls (Anik and Enid) share this three-prong longer tail

4. Florian's fluffy loop stitch tail is shared with Kevin, Tricia and Elizabeth

5. Gareth's short and shapely tail is shared with Ben and Huck

6. Duke has a small pointed tail that you sew your yarn end through once it is in position to create a curl

7. Jack has a unique dual-layered tail made in two parts

8. Celine has a short dual-layered flared tail made in two parts

9. Caesar, Petra and Oscar share this rear view

10. Margot has a sophisticated shapely tail perfectly matched to her wings

11. Rohit's waiting to fully grow into his magnificent three-part tail

12. Kit's glorious tail makes the most of the slip stitch

13. Ross's glorious two-part tail takes a bit of concentration so keep a check on your colour changes, but is definitely worth it

14. Hazel's tail is perfectly proportioned to her body and uses the chain loop technique

15. Gilbert's tail is sew in an alert position by just sewing a couple of stitches up the back either side of the tail

ABOUT THE AUTHOR

Kerry Lord is the founder and creative director behind the TOFT luxury yarn brand.
Kerry and her company have been a loud voice in the UK craft revival years since 2006.

She lives with her family in Leamington Spa, Warwickshire.

www.toftuk.com

THANK YOU

Thanks to Edward Lord, born September 2012, who becomes more of an inspiration every day.

I would like to mention baby Reuben (and his geeky mum), who arrived at exactly the right time to renew my energy and enthusiasm for this project.

I would also like to thank the following people for all their help in crocheting various experimental awkward parts often at short notice:

Caroline Corner, Emily Steeden, Emma Brown, Liz Kidner, Petra Baker

Then of course there's my husband Doug who deserves endless thanks for tolerating relentless ornithological facts, stuffing tasks and occasionally finding bits of yarn in his dinner over the last six months.

SUPPLIERS

All the animals in the *Edward's Menagerie* collection of mammals and birds are made using TOFT yarns in fine, double knitting, aran and chunky weights. TOFT yarns are made in the UK and are characterized by a predominantly all-natural colour palette. With the creation of *Edward's Menagerie: Birds*, TOFT now manufactures the six dyed shades needed to complete all the birds featured in this book. Only the highest-quality natural fibres are selected for use in TOFT yarns to ensure they are a pleasure to work with and will guarantee a stunning look and feel in your completed project.

For how-to videos, workshops and to purchase TOFT yarns to accompany this book visit:

www.toftuk.com

To find international stockists of TOFT yarns and kits see the website for details.

INDEX

A DAVID AND CHARLES BOOK
© David and Charles, Ltd 2015

David and Charles is an imprint of David and Charles, Ltd
Suite A, Tourism House, Pynes Hill, Exeter, EX2 5WS

Text and Designs © Kerry Lord
Layout and Photography © David and Charles, Ltd 2015

First published in the UK and USA in 2015

A catalogue record for this book is available from the British Library.

ISBN-13: 978-1-4463-0602-4 paperback
ISBN-13: 978-1-4463-7264-7 EPUB

This book has been printed on paper from approved suppliers and made from pulp
from sustainable sources.

Printed in China by Leo for:
David and Charles, Ltd
Suite A, Tourism House, Pynes Hill, Exeter, EX2 5WS

10

Acquisitions Editor: Ame Verso
Managing Editor: Honor Head
Project Editor: Jane Trollope
Pattern checker: Lynne Rowe
Art Editor: Anna Fazakerley
Designers: Matthew Lilly, Lorraine Inglis
Photographer: Jason Jenkins
Production Manager: Beverley Richardson

David and Charles publishes high-quality books on a wide range of subjects.
For more information visit www.davidandcharles.com.

Share your makes with us on social media using #dandcbooks and follow us on
Facebook and Instagram by searching for @dandcbooks.

Layout of the digital edition of this book may vary depending on reader hardware
and display settings.